PRINCIPLES OF
TEXT PROCESSING

F. N. TESKEY, B.A., M.A., Ph.D.
Department of Computer Science
University of Manchester

ELLIS HORWOOD LIMITED
Publishers · Chichester

Halsted Press: a division of
JOHN WILEY & SONS
New York · Brisbane · Chichester · Toronto

First published in 1982 by

ELLIS HORWOOD LIMITED
Market Cross House, Cooper Street, Chichester, West Sussex, PO19 1EB, England

The publisher's colophon is reproduced from James Gillison's drawing of the ancient Market Cross, Chichester.

Distributors:

Australia, New Zealand, South-east Asia:
Jacaranda-Wiley Ltd., Jacaranda Press,
JOHN WILEY & SONS INC.,
G.P.O. Box 859, Brisbane, Queensland 40001, Australia

Canada:
JOHN WILEY & SONS CANADA LIMITED
22 Worcester Road, Rexdale, Ontario, Canada.

Europe, Africa:
JOHN WILEY & SONS LIMITED
Baffins Lane, Chichester, West Sussex, England.

North and South America and the rest of the world:
Halsted Press: a division of
JOHN WILEY & SONS
605 Third Avenue, New York, N.Y. 10016, U.S.A.

©1982 F. N. Teskey/Ellis Horwood Ltd.

British Library Cataloguing in Publication Data
Teskey, F. N.
Principles of text processing. –
(Ellis Horwood series in computers and their applications)
1. Word processing (Office practice)
2. Electronic data processing
I. Title
001.64   HF5547.5

Library of Congress Card No. 82-2906 AACR2

ISBN 0-85312-264-4 (Ellis Horwood Limited, Publishers – Library Edn.)
ISBN 0-85312-446-9 (Ellis Horwood Limited, Publishers – Student Edn.)
ISBN 0-470-27335-6 (Halsted Press)

Typeset in Press Roman by Ellis Horwood Ltd.
Printed in Great Britain by R. J. Acford, Chichester.

PRINCIPLES OF TEXT PROCESSING

THE ELLIS HORWOOD SERIES IN
COMPUTERS AND THEIR APPLICATIONS

Series Editor: BRIAN MEEK
Director of the Computer Unit, Queen Elizabeth College, University of London

The series aims to provide up-to-date and readable texts on the theory and practice of computing, with particular though not exclusive emphasis on computer applications. Preference is given in planning the series to new or developing areas, or to new approaches in established areas.

 The books will usually be at the level of introductory or advanced undergraduate courses. In most cases they will be suitable as course texts, with their use in industrial and commercial fields always kept in mind. Together they will provide a valuable nucleus for a computing science library.

INTERACTIVE COMPUTER GRAPHICS IN SCIENCE TEACHING
Edited by J. McKENZIE, University College, London, L. ELTON, University of Surrey, R. LEWIS, Chelsea College, London.
INTRODUCTORY ALGOL 68 PROGRAMMING
D. F. BRAILSFORD and A. N. WALKER, University of Nottingham.
GUIDE TO GOOD PROGRAMMING PRACTICE
Edited by B. L. MEEK, Queen Elizabeth College, London and P. HEATH, Plymouth Polytechnic.
CLUSTER ANALYSIS ALGORITHMS: For Data Reduction and Classification of Objects
H. SPÄTH, Professor of Mathematics, Oldenburg University.
DYNAMIC REGRESSION: Theory and Algorithms
L. J. SLATER, Department of Applied Engineering, Cambridge University and
H. M. PESARAN, Trinity College, Cambridge
FOUNDATIONS OF PROGRAMMING WITH PASCAL
LAWRIE MOORE, Birkbeck College, London.
PROGRAMMING LANGUAGE STANDARDISATION
Edited by B. L. MEEK, Queen Elizabeth College, London and I. D. HILL, Clinical Research Centre, Harrow.
THE DARTMOUTH TIME SHARING SYSTEM
G. M. BULL, The Hatfield Polytechnic
RECURSIVE FUNCTIONS IN COMPUTER SCIENCE
R. PETER, formerly Eötvos Lorand University of Budapest.
FUNDAMENTALS OF COMPUTER LOGIC
D. HUTCHISON, University of Strathclyde.
THE MICROCHIP AS AN APPROPRIATE TECHNOLOGY
Dr. A. BURNS, The Computing Laboratory, Bradford University
SYSTEMS ANALYSIS AND DESIGN FOR COMPUTER APPLICATION
D. MILLINGTON, University of Strathclyde.
COMPUTING USING BASIC: An Interactive Approach
TONIA COPE, Oxford University Computing Teaching Centre.
RECURSIVE DESCENT COMPILING
A. J. T. DAVIE and R. MORRISON, University of St. Andrews, Scotland.
PASCAL IMPLEMENTATION
S. PEMBERTON and M. DANIELS, Brighton Polytechnic
MICROCOMPUTERS IN EDUCATION
Edited by I. C. H. SMITH, Queen Elizabeth College, University of London
AN INTRODUCTION TO PROGRAMMING LANGUAGE TRANSITION
R. E. BERRY, University of Lancaster
ADA: A PROGRAMMER'S CONVERSION COURSE
M. J. STRATFORD-COLLINS, U.S.A.
STRUCTURED PROGRAMMING WITH COMAL
R. ATHERTON, Bulmershe College of Higher Education
SOFTWARE ENGINEERING
K. GEWALD, G. HAAKE and W. PFADLER, Siemens AG, Munich

Table of Contents

Chapter 8 – The Next Generation of Text Processing Systems

Author's Preface

Whilst the use of text based information systems has been increasing in recent years, descriptions of the principles on which these systems are based are distributed amongst a number of sources. The aim of this book is to gather together this material, present it in a unified form and establish the basic principles underlying the use of computers in text processing. In the early stages of this book, the phrase 'text processing' was adopted more by accident than design. As the book evolved, the phrase became increasingly appropriate, and so it has been retained. It is intended to cover both information retrieval and data base management systems, without putting undue emphasis on either. The book is intended primarily as a text book for undergraduate and postgraduate students in computer and information science; though it is hoped that it will be useful to the practitioners as well as the students of information processing. There are a large number of techniques that are used in developing information processing systems. I have concentrated on those that are relevant to text based systems and have omitted a number of peripheral topics. The reader should be able to find more details of these from the references in the bibliography.

I am very grateful to Bryan Niblett who, not only introduced me to the subject of information retrieval systems, but also suggested that I should write a book on the subject. I started writing the book whilst I was working for the UK Atomic Energy Authority on the STATUS project; I wish to thank the Authority for the encouragement they provided, as well as for permission to publish the material on STATUS, which forms the core of Chapter 7. I completed the book whilst working in the Computer Science Department of the University of Manchester, and I am very grateful for the support given by the University.

I should like to express my thanks to Brian Meek for his very helpful comments on the initial drafts of each chapter and to Richard Jones, Ron Mount and Simon Lavington for their comments on the final manuscript. I am indebted to Mrs. Cathy Knight for typing the manuscript; finally, I want to thank my wife, not only for all her help in proof-reading, but also for her interest and encouragement whilst I have been working on this book.

F. N. Teskey
October 1981

1

Introduction

*Well now, shall we not walk
and seek together?*

Kahlil Gibran
The Wanderer

1.1 THE AIMS OF TEXT PROCESSING SYSTEMS

As the structure of our society becomes increasingly complex, individuals and groups need to communicate an expanding volume of information. Much of this information is transferred as text, but the accummulation of large volumes of text intensifies the problem of identifying relevant material. The aim of a text processing system is to organise and control large volumes of text so that they can be used for the efficient communication of information. Also, as the amount of text increases and the number of people who want access to the text increases, then simple manual processes become ineffective and there is a need for more efficient, automated text processing systems.

A text processing system has a number of functions which it must support. Firstly it must be able to collect text from a variety of sources; these sources may be distributed across a wide geographical area and may be producing text in a number of different formats on a number of different media. It is often far from trivial to collate all this data into a standard form at a single location. Secondly the system must provide storage for all this text. Storing large volumes of text can, in itself, be a problem, but there is no point in storing the text if we cannot gain access to it. This brings us to the third requirement, namely the ability to retrieve specified data from the stored text. Finally a text processing system should have the capability to process the retrieved text and present it to the user in an acceptable format. This whole process can be represented in Fig. 1.1 In the simplest case (a) there is just a single source and a single user and they are in direct communication. In the next case (b) there is still just a single source and user but they are no longer in direct communication. The source has stored a certain amount of text in the data base and the user can request to see any of

(a)   direct transfer

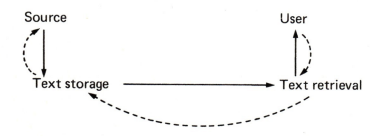

(b)   single user system

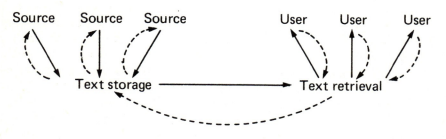

(c)   multi-user system

⟶ flow of text

----► request for information

Fig. 1.1 – Stages in the development of a text-processing system.
(a) direct transfer; (b) single user system; (c) multi user system.

this information. Requests for information not already in the data base are passed back to the source and may result in the required text being added to the system. This last link, the storage system requesting new text from the source, is often very weak. Finally (c) represents the general multi-source multi-user environment that is typical of most automated text processing systems. Here a variety of sources are contributing to a single text store and this is being accessed by a number of different users.

To summarise, text processing systems are intended to facilitate the transfer of textual information between a group of sources and a group of users. Such a system consists of:

    (i) a number of text sources
   (ii) a means of storing text
  (iii) a means of extracting information from the stored text
  (iv) a group of users.

Each user should be able to request and receive information from the system just as he would from the original source.

1.2 THE AIMS OF THIS BOOK

This book aims to describe some of the principles of computerised text processing and show how these can be used in the design of text based information systems. The basic concepts are illustrated by examples and, where appropriate, by simple algorithms. These are intended to give the reader a general idea of how text processing systems operate, without going into the detailed workings of individual systems. Where appropriate, complex techniques are described only in outline with references to primary sources. Some of the various methods used in text processing are brought together in the description of a single integrated system and illustrated by a few of its applications. The book concludes with a review of current work in the field of text processing, and some thoughts on the impact these will have on the next generation of text processing systems.

As well as describing the principles of text processing, the book aims to show the range of applications of free text systems. The traditional view is that free text systems are applicable only to bibliographic and closely related areas. Our view is that there is a much wider range of applications, including many, such as personnel records, that have traditionally been regarded as the preserve of data base management systems (DBMS). Highlighting these applications, and the limitations of existing free text systems in these areas, should help in the development of more comprehensive text processing systems.

The book assumes little prior knowledge of the subject. It is assumed that the reader is familiar with the basic concepts of computing and with simple algorithms written with a PASCAL-like control structure. The use of mathematics has been kept to a minimum. Two notations that may be unfamiliar are:

(i) $\Sigma\, a_i$ to indicate the sum of values a_1, a_2, a_3 etc.

(ii) $\{x:p(x)\}$ to indicate the set of elements x such that the proposition $p(x)$ is true.

The discussions on text analysis require only a limited understanding of the fundamentals of English grammar.

The book is aimed, not only at the student of information science, but also towards the growing number of people now working in the field of information. This includes not only those involved in designing and building information systems, but also those responsible for implementing and maintaining such systems, as well as the end users. Any job that involves dealing with a substantial quantity of text has a potential for using an automated text processing system. Libraries are one of the first areas that spring to mind, but lawyers, doctors and other professions all have large volumes of text to handle. Though there is a great potential for text processing systems, the current systems are too expensive for many applications. If sufficient people become aware of the techniques that are available then there is more likelihood of developing systems that are suitable for many more of these applications.

1.3 THE SCOPE OF THIS BOOK

This book is aimed at a number of different groups of people and so the scope and coverage of individual areas may not be as detailed as individual readers might require. It would be impossible in a book of this size to provide a complete coverage of all aspects of text processing systems, what we have attempted to do is to present a balanced introduction to the subject.

For the student of information science the book describes the basic principles of text processing systems. It covers not only the concepts of information storage and retrieval but also the problems of the user interface and data base management. Though some time is spent looking at the next generation of text processing systems there is no attempt to provide a complete review of current research or even the current state of the art.

For the systems designer, the book gathers together some of the algorithms that have been used or described in the literature. These are not intended to provide the nucleus for some new system but rather to highlight some of the problem areas and to indicate possible solutions. There is a great tendency when writing programs to 'reinvent the wheel' rather than adopt existing algorithms and programs. This tendency becomes much more serious when one is considering designing and building a new system. The book contains a discussion of the use of software packages in text processing systems, and aims to show that it is not necessary to build such information systems from scratch for each new application.

One chapter of the book is devoted to the data base manager. The problems and responsibilities of data administration are discussed in detail. The rest of the book, however, should also be relevant to the data base manager; in particular he should be able to obtain background information on what types of facilities are available to meet his particular requirements.

Finally we come to the end user. Though he has no need to know the detailed working of the system he is using, he may be able to make better use of the system if he has some understanding of the principles on which it operates. Because of some details of design or implementation, a system may be able to perform one task easily and efficiently whilst another very similar task is difficult or impossible. This type of situation can be very confusing to the user and the information necessary to appreciate the problem is not often presented in the user manual or other system documentation. The interested user should be able to find some of this information in this book.

1.4 THE HISTORY OF TEXT PROCESSING

The earliest known forms of writing date from 3500 BC. Since then man has been collecting and storing written documents. One of the major collections of documents in the classical world was the library at Alexandria. This was started by Ptolemy II Philadelphus in about 260 BC, it was intended that it should hold copies of all the important manuscripts in the known world and at its height it held over 700,000 rolls. The library could, perhaps, be called one of the first information centres. In its time it was indeed a centre of learning, but after the Moslems captured Alexandria, Caliph Omar, afraid of the effect of this learning on the Moslem world, ordered the destruction of the library in 649 AD. Now all that remains is a small fragment of the ruins.

Before the introduction of printing there were few large libraries, but this changed once printing became established. The first use of printing in Europe is commonly attributed to Gutenberg in 1454, though it is likely that printing in China predates this by over 600 years. The early presses were undoubtedly very slow and primitive, but with the advent of machines that could print hundreds of copies a minute the written word was readily available.

With the spread of printing came the beginning of the information explosion. It was no longer possible for any one man to be aware of all the books that had been published – it was necessary to bring some sort of order into the increasing volume of printed books. One of the first, and still widely used, types of book classification was that developed by Dewey in 1876. This system is based on the decimal notation and divides all human knowledge into ten major fields; each of these is subdivided into a hundred subsidiary fields and these can be split into finer classifications if required; this is illustrated in Fig. 1.2. This system has worked well and is still in wide-spread use, but it does suffer from a number of limitations. Firstly it relies on intellectual effort to assign a classification number to each book – as the number of books increases this becomes more and more expensive. Secondly, and more seriously, a reader will find a particular book on a given topic only if that topic has a classification number and if the person classifying the book thought that the number was the most appropriate. Some more complex schemes allow more than one code to be assigned to a single document. Indeed, this is apparent to a limited extent in the standard Dewey codes. In the example given in Fig. 1.2 we see that 700 is art, 900 is history and so 709 is history of art, 73 is the code for the United States and so 709.73 is the history of art in the United States. The problem with this approach is that although all the documents dealing with, for example, the United States have a common sub-code, the individual codes are scattered throughout the whole system.

500	Science
540	Chemistry and allied sciences
541	Physical and theoretical chemistry
541.2	Theoretical chemistry
541.3	Physical chemistry
541.34	Solutions
541.35	Photochemistry
542	Laboratories, apparatus, equipment
.	
.	
.	
700	The arts
709	History of art
709.73	History of art in the United States
.	
.	
.	
900	General geography and history
970	History of North America
973	History of the United States

Fig. 1.2 – Part of the Dewey Classification Scheme.

The Dewey classification scheme was not suitable for some special technical libraries and an alternative was necessary. One simple method is the edge notched card. Details of each document in the collection are typed on a card as shown in Fig. 1.3. Each document can have a number of different index terms assigned to it, each index term corresponds to one of the numbered holes round the edge of the card. In the card illustrated there is scope for up to 50 different index terms, though this could be increased for larger cards. If a given index term has been assigned to a document, then the corresponding perforated notch is removed from the edge of the card, so in the example terms 2 and 3 have been assigned

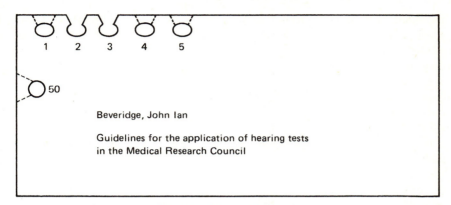

Fig. 1.3 -- Edge notched card.

to the document. If a user then wants to find all documents with both index terms 2 and 3, he can take all the cards, push a rod through holes 2 and 3, lift up the cards by these rods and the cards containing the required documents will drop out. This method is effective but obviously has severe limitations on the number of index terms and the number of documents that can be processed, now the use of computers has allowed the processing of much larger volumes of text.

Most of the earliest uses of computers were for numerical calculations; it was some time before any work was done on the use of computers to store and retrieve text. There was, initially, some thought that computers could provide a complete solution to all the problems of text processing — analysing and storing text, answering questions, translating from one language to another etc. etc. Luhn (1957) presented a more realistic approach; he identified a spectrum of types of information needed and discussed how computers might be used to meet these needs. The simplest types of system were based on the occurrence of keywords, in effect a computerised version of the edge notched cards. Since then, countless text processing systems, offering a wide range of facilities, have been developed; some of these systems are in production supporting many thousands of users, while others are experimental systems that are unlikely to emerge from the laboratory for many years. In the remainder of this book we will attempt to describe the main features of some of these systems.

1.5 THE SOCIAL IMPACT OF TEXT PROCESSING SYSTEMS

As the use of text processing systems increases there is a growing concern about the impact such systems will have on society. Before discussing this in detail it is worth looking at it from an historical point of view. The introduction of computerised text processing has many similarities with the introduction of printing 500 years earlier. At that time the use of books was almost entirely in the preserve of the church, so the use of printing appeared to be limited to the Bible and other religious works. Also these manuscripts were copied by the scribes in the church and the use of printing threatened their jobs. The introduction of printing could well have been opposed on these grounds. What, in fact, happened was the creation of a whole new market for the written word and, though the job of copying manuscripts disappeared, many new jobs were created. It is interesting to speculate whether similar comments were made on the introduction of writing 5,000 years earlier.

The view still persists that information retrieval systems will be used only in libraries and that they will make librarians redundant. It seems very probable that what happened with printing 500 years ago will also happen with computerised text processing systems today. As systems are developed they will open up new markets for themselves and, though many of the traditional library jobs will disappear, there will be a need for many more new jobs. It is very difficult to predict what these new applications and new jobs will be. It is likely that in time every business will find a need for a computerised text processing system, just as now it has a need for a typewriter; it is possible, but less certain, that households will come to regard a personal text processing system as essential as, say, a telephone.

There is another, more serious, concern about the growing use of text processing systems, and that is privacy. In a democratic society people have come to expect a certain degree of privacy from the attention both of the state and of other citizens. The agents of the state have, for a long time kept records of people in whom they are interested. These files will, in general, have been set up for one particular purpose and can be used only for that purpose. For example a regional health centre may set up a file containing all the medical records for people in that area, and that file can be used only to retrieve the medical record of each given patient. Since the individual knows that any information he is providing is just for his medical record and will be seen only by medical staff, he can feel confident that his privacy is not being invaded. The situation changes, however, when computerised systems are introduced. Once the data is stored in machine readable form it becomes practical to gain access to it in ways other than that which was originally intended. So to continue our previous example, while it would be possible to manually search through the file of medical records to find, say, all unmarried mothers in a given town, the size of the task makes it almost impossible. Once the data is on a computer, then searches such as these are much easier and the patient may well feel that his privacy has been invaded. As we shall see, free text systems are particularly vulnerable to this type of abuse, and it is essential that adequate safeguards should be maintained.

As with most scientific and technical inventions, the social problems of information systems come from the use of the system rather than the system itself. As an illustration of this, most people would welcome the use of computerised free text systems to help the police deal with, for example, a major murder inquiry but many would object to the use of the same system for day-to-day surveillance of whole sections of the population. It is the responsibility of the scientist to explain to society the benefits and dangers of his invention, but society at large must accept responsibility for how the invention is used.

This brings us to the last point in the discussion of the social impact of text processing systems, namely user education. As computerised information systems become more widely available, so more people will have to learn how to use them. Once again, the situation has similarities with the introduction of printing; at that time the availability of printed books led to an increase in the number of people who could read. At present, training in the use of computerised information systems seems limited to a few higher education courses and technical courses organised by the vendors of the individual systems. There is no immediate prospect of the introduction of intelligent information systems, requiring no particular expertise to use; so if the growth of text processing systems is to be maintained there must be a substantial programme of user education.

1.6 TYPES OF TEXT PROCESSING SYSTEMS

So far we have discussed various aspects of text processing in general, but in fact there is a whole range of different types of systems each with their own characteristics. We can classify text processing systems either by the type of function they perform or by the algorithms they use, The functions of a text processing system can be divided into the following three classes:

  (i) Document retrieval
  (ii) Data retrieval
  (iii) Question answering.

Document retrieval is the basic library function of identifying books and articles that may be relevant to a particular reader's request, for example, a request for material relating to the use of information retrieval systems in keeping dental patient records. The function of data retrieval systems is to extract individual pieces of information from a data base in response to a specific request, for example, the use of a data base of vehicle registration numbers and registered keepers, to find the keeper of a given vehicle. Finally, question answering systems aim to provide expert information in a given subject field, in response to questions asked in natural language. This is similar to data retrieval, the main difference is that the system is interrogated in natural language, and it must have the ability to make complex deductions in order to obtain an answer to the user's question.

These three types of system can be represented diagrammatically as in Fig. 1.4. In all cases the user has an information need and a data base which should satisfy that need. In the document retrieval system, the user has a question

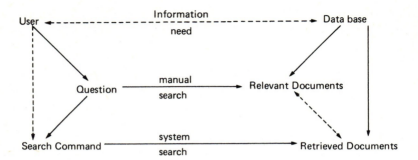

(a)   document retrieval

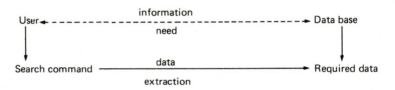

(b)   data retrieval

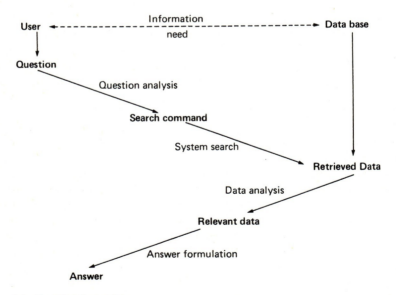

(c)   Question Answering

Fig. 1.4 — Types of text processing systems.
(a) document retrieval; (b) data retrieval; (c) question answering.

and he believes that a manual search through the entire data base would produce some relevant documents. The user then transforms this question into a search command, the system executes the search and retrieves a set of documents, hopefully relevant ones. In a data retrieval system the user's question is such that it can be expressed directly as a search request, (or in a very similar form) this can be processed by the system to extract the required information from the data base. Finally, in a question answering system, the system itself analyses the user's question to produce a search command, the retrieved data is analysed to produce the data required and this is then presented to the user as an answer to his original question.

As an alternative to this classification we propose a definition of complete or closed systems.

1.6.1 Definition
A text processing system is closed if and only if it has:

(i) a well defined set of sources and users
(ii) a well defined set of information requests
(iii) an algorithm to extract the required data for each type of information request.

A text processing system is open if and only if it is not closed. □

1.6.2 Example
An example of a closed system is a car registration data base for standard British number plates, which:

(i) takes its input from the registration documents completed by car owners
(ii) is to be used only by the police
(iii) is to be used only to determine the registered keeper of a car with a given registration number. □

In general data retrieval systems will be closed while document retrieval systems will be open, though it is possible to imagine small closed document systems. The problems of open systems are more demanding because the system must have some means, however crude, of extracting the meaning of the source text and relating it to the user's request. The philosophical distinction between intentional and extentional theories of meaning can be carried over into the classification of text processing systems.

1.6.3 Definition
A text processing system is intentional if an only if it has some 'world view' to which it can relate the intent of the source text.

A text processing system is extentional if and only if it has some concept of the extent of application of individual words which it can use in the analysis of the source text. □

1.6.4 Example
The Dewey classification scheme can be regarded as intentional since it relates each text to a given classification number in its view of all human knowledge. Free text systems are extentional since, as we shall see, they rely on the extent of occurrence of individual words. □

As we said earlier we can also classify text processing systems by the types of algorithms that they use. In the succeeding chapters of this book we will outline some of these algorithms. The algorithms used for retrieval can be divided into two main classes:

(i) Pattern matching – from the user's request for data the system decides what type of data he wants and tries to find some similar information in the data base, for example, Boolean, term weighting, etc.
(ii) Goal searching – the system looks for data from which it can construct, calculate or deduce an answer to the user's question, for example, relational systems, question answering systems, etc.

This distinction should become clearer as we discuss the individual algorithms in more detail.

1.7 OUTLINE OF THE BASIC FUNCTIONS
Despite the variation in different types of text processing they all have a number of basic functions in common. These functions can be summarised as:
(i) text analysis
(ii) data storage
(iii) data extraction
(iv) user interface
(v) data management.

These five functions are central to all text processing systems, indeed their implementation determines the implementation of the whole system. The reader will have observed that they correspond to the areas covered by Chapters 2-6 of this book. Before we go on to look at each of them in detail it is worthwhile to explain briefly the purpose of each function.

A text processing systems contains, as we said in section 1.1, a number of text sources. This text will normally be presented to the system as a sequence of characters and some type of analysis is required to transform it into a form that can be used by the rest of the system. The depth of this analysis determines the detail of information that can eventually be obtained from the system. So if the analysis does no more than identify the occurrence of certain key words then the only information that can be supplied is a list of documents containing given keywords. While, if the analysis extracts some of the meaning of the source text then this information is available to help answer the user's question. We will see that the intentional systems tend to provide a deep analysis of a small subject area while the extentional systems provide a less detailed analysis of a much wider area.

The second constituent of a text processing system is a means of storing the source text. It is equally important to be able to store the analysed text. (For brevity we will often refer to the source text and the analysed text as text and data respectively.) The storage of the source text is common to all types of system but the storage of analysed text will depend on the format of the data, and this, in turn, will be determined by the type of analysis that has been used. Whatever type of storage is used, the principal requirement is that the rest of the system should have easy access to all the data.

The third constituent of a text processing system is a means of extracting data from the stored data base. The data to be extracted could be anything from a single numerical value to a large set of documents, and the data may be directly relevant to the user's question or may require further processing before being presented to the user. The methods used for extracting data will depend very heavily on the type of analysis and data storage that have been employed.

The last constituent of a text processing system that was mentioned in section 1.1 is the user group. The user must have some means of communicating with the rest of the system and this function is performed by the user interface. If the system is to work efficiently then the user interface must be carefully engineered to match the computer algorithms on the one hand with the abilities and requirements of the user group on the other hand. For the inexperienced user the interface should be designed to lead him through a well-defined sequence of operations, whilst the experienced user will require a more powerful, flexible interface.

In our original list of constituents of a text processing system we did not mention the requirement for data management. In any system there will be a need to exercise some control over the content and use of the data base. This is required not only to ensure the privacy and security of any information in the system, but also to maintain its validity and integrity. This is discussed in more detail in Chapter 6.

The remaining Chapters, 7 and 8, contain discussions of two further areas. Chapter 7 introduces the concept of integrated systems, that is looking at the whole aspect of information transfer from source to user as a single system. This is illustrated by a description of one such system and a number of its applications. Lastly, Chapter 8 presents a personal view of some of the current research in the field of information systems and some thoughts on the next generation of text processing systems.

1.8 EXPERIMENTAL AND PRODUCTION SYSTEMS

Though the history of text processing systems extends over only a few decades, there are already a large number of experimental and production systems in existence. The experimental systems can be divided into two major areas, those trying to improve the performance of document retrieval systems and those trying to increase the scope of question answering systems.

A document retrieval system produces a set of retrieved documents which, ideally, should be identical to the set of relevant documents. We will see later that one way of measuring the performance of such systems is to compare these two sets, and many experimental systems have been developed to study ways of improving this aspect of performance. Some significant improvements have been made but, as yet, no substantial gains have been achieved; the performance, measured in these terms, still remains low. Part of the problem with this type of experimental system is that the definition of relevance is very subjective. To overcome this limitation it is necessary to measure the performance of the system over a large range of users, questions and application areas — this, needless to say, is very expensive and outside the scope of most experimental systems. There are other aspects of performance that are now receiving attention. In particular, the user interface has a significant impact on the efficiency of the whole system and experimental systems are being developed to study this and other aspects of performance.

We mentioned that question answering systems tended to be restricted to a small well defined subject area. The reasons for this are to ensure that the source text can be comprehensively analysed, and to allow the construction of a sufficiently detailed 'world view' of the subject area. From very modest beginnings these systems have expanded to cover wider and wider subject areas, but it is still not clear if they will ever cover a sufficiently wide subject area to make them practical and useful systems.

As well as the basic research on experimental systems, there is also a considerable amount of work devoted to the design, development, maintenance and improvement of production text processing systems. These systems are used to serve two types of user groups:

    (i) public
    (ii) in-house.

The public systems aim to provide a service to any member of the general public who is prepared to pay for the particular service. This originated with offering a document retrieval service to the scientific community and has now developed into a major industry. There are several different services available, the largest offering over 100 different data bases and the largest data bases containing bibliographic details of over a million documents; the subjects covered range from agriculture to zoology. As well as these multi-disciplinary systems there are also a growing number of specialised systems to meet the needs of particular groups such as lawyers, accountants etc. By aiming at a more limited user group, these systems are able to provide a service that is more closely matched to the user's requirements. The public information service has recently seen the introduction of viewdata systems. These are intended to provide an information service to the public at large, though at present the main use seems to be in service industries such as travel agents, banks etc. The system is based on a hierarchical index and allows the user to browse through pages of textual and graphic information.

In contrast to the public systems, the in-house systems are used to provide a service to a group of users within a single organisation. In the UK alone it is estimated (Ashford and Matkin 1980) that there are over 8,000 centres with an actual or potential requirement for information management and retrieval systems. The type of systems in use or required are largely document and data retrieval systems for bibliographic references, personnel records, technical reports etc. As we mentioned earlier, question answering systems are not yet sufficiently well developed for production use. One system was used in earnest by a group of geologists investigating lunar rock samples (Woods *et al.* 1972). The results of this project tend to confirm the view that such question answering systems are not yet sufficiently well developed for production use.

1.9 INFORMATION THEORY AND LINGUISTICS

Before we begin a detailed study of the principles and methods of text processing, it is worthwhile taking a brief look at two neighbouring disciplines, information theory and linguistics, to see what impact they may have on our present study.

The concepts of information theory were first outlined by Shannon (1949). He was concerned with the problem of communicating information in the presence of noise, and produced formulae for the maximum rate of transmission of binary digits over a system with various types of noise. These results are very important in the field of communication but the use of the word 'information' tends to imply that the theory has a wider range of application. In fact the theory deals only with the quantity of information and makes no attempt to assess the quality or meaning of the information; this is illustrated by a simple example. Consider sending the following message over a noisy system:

> "Having a wonderful time, wish you were here."

As far as information theory is concerned, the following two incorrect versions have suffered the same loss of information, but the loss or change of meaning is quite different:

> "Having a wonderful tim, wish you were here."
> "Having a wonderful time, wish you were her."

In its present form information theory offers little help in solving the problems of text processing systems.

The study of linguistics seems more likely to influence the development of text processing systems. The theories of grammar developed by Chomsky (1964) and others has led directly to the design of computer systems capable of understanding simple English sentences. A text processing system, however, must be capable of understanding not only short sentences but also long passages of text, and this has proved a very difficult linguistic problem. As yet, the study of linguistics has provided little information to help with building a 'world view' for use in intentional systems.

The particular problems of text processing systems tend to be distinct from those related dsciplines. Information theory provides a specific means of measuring the quantity of information but provides no indication of the quality of that information. On the other hand, linguistics provides the tools to perform a detailed analysis of individual sentences but gives little guidance on extracting information from large quantities of text. A text processing system needs some measure of the relevance of quality of information and a deductive capability that can deal with large volumes of text. Neither information theory nor liguistics can, at present, answer these problems. In the remainder of this book we will see how some aspects of these problems can be tackled from an information engineering point of view.

2

Text Analysis

2.1 TYPES OF ANALYSIS

A text processing system, as defined in Chapter 1, must contain a means of retrieving data from the text stored in the system. To perform this function, in anything other than a trivial manner, requires some form of text analysis. The aim of this type of analysis is to convert the text into a form that can be readily processed by a computer and so provide an effective means of retrieving data. This chapter describes some of the algorithms that can be used for this type of analysis.

It is possible to base an analysis of textual material on any one of a number of different levels of description. If the text is presented verbally then the analysis would naturally be based on the description of the sound waves and this leads to the study of voice recognition. Similarly if the text is presented in printed form then the analysis would start with the patterns of ink on the page — optical character recognition. Both these fields however, lie outside the scope of this book and a fuller description can be found in Lea (1980) or Anderson (1976); instead we shall start with the next level of description, the character. At this level of description the text is regarded as a string of characters (including spaces and punctuation marks), this is a more abstract level and so has greater independence of the original form of representation. This type of description is particularly suited to digital computer systems since each of the individual characters can be represented internally by a unique bit string, it is widely used for storing textual material and will be used throughout the rest of this book.

In any natural language text it is obvious that sequences of characters are combined into words, sequences of words are combined into sentences, and that those sentences convey the meaning of the text. This gives rise to a hierarchy of levels of descriptions:

(i) Lexical
(ii) Syntactic
(iii) Semantic

and associated types of analysis. Thus we can define a lexical analyser as one which takes a string of characters and identifies the individual words in the input; similarly a syntactic analyser takes this string of words and identifies the individual sentences, (and the implicit grammatical relations); finally a semantic analyser takes these sentences and identifies some of the meaning of the text.

A text processing system will, in general, handle not only natural language but other types of textual material as well. Examples of such data whould be chemical formulae, car registrations, names and addresses. Such text will still need to be analysed and, where it is possible, it is useful to extend the definition of the above types of analysis to all textual material. Thus any text processing system will contain at least one of these forms of analysis and so we can classify these systems according to the level of textual analysis that they perform.

2.2 LEXICAL ANALYSIS

A text processing system must deal with some physical representation of the text and as indicated in the last section, we shall take the character string representation as standard. So, given a finite set of characters a text string is defined as a sequence of these characters. A typical set of characters that might be used is:

(i) the letters A–Z
(ii) the digits 0–9
(iii) The punctuation marks and special characters , . : ; - + etc.
and (iv) the space character denoted by ⌃.

Using this set of characters the following is a text string

THIS⌃IS⌃A⌃TEXT⌃STRING.

In this example, it is obvious what the individual words are and we can formalise our intuitive lexical analysis as follows.

2.2.1 Definition

A word is a finite sequence of letters delimited by spaces or punctuation marks. □

This definition, however, is both too restrictive in that it does not allow words with special characters (such as 'CO-OP), and too general in that it regards related words (such as 'CAT' and its plural 'CATS') as quite distinct. In the rest of this section we shall look at ways of overcoming these problems.

The problem of special characters can be partially overcome by the introduction of the notion of **concordable** characters. (Literally those characters that can occur in words in an index or **concordance**.) These are the characters that can be used to form valid words. There are, however, some characters that can only occur in certain circumstances, for example if a hyphen occurs in the middle of a word then it should be regarded as part of that word while if it occurs at the end of a line of text it can be ignored. These type of characters are called **optionally concordable**, the remainder are **non-concordable**. So with these three types of characters:

(i) concordable for example A–Z, 0–9
(ii) optionally concordable for example - .
(iii) non-concordable for example ^ ! ?

we can formulate a second definition of a word.

2.2.2 Definition
A word is a finite sequence of concordable and optionally concordable characters delimited by either a non-concordable character or an optionally concordable character adjacent to a non-concordable or optionally concordable one. □

2.2.3 Example
Given the above set of characters and definition the text string

   ^ C O - O P ^ 1 9 8 0 . ^ 1 9 8 . 0 ^

contains the three words

   'CO-OP' '1980' and '198.0' □

The definition of section 2.2.2 can be formalised using the Backus–Naur form (BNF). The simplest form of BNF consists of two (metalinguistic) symbols which have the following meaning:

   ::=   definition
   | logical OR

So for example

   a::= b|c

signifies that an entity of type 'a' must be either of type 'b' or of type 'c'. The power of the notation comes from the ease of representation of recursive definitions. Thus:

   W ::= c|cW

implies that W is either of type 'c' or 'c' followed by a valid W, that is 'c', 'cc', 'ccc' etc. In the formal use of BNF (metalinguistic) variables are enclosed in angled brackets, thus $<w>$; this is described in detail by Backus (1960). Using the simple notation the definition of a word is as follows.

2.2.4 Definition
The set **W** of valid word is

$$W:: = \quad c \mid cW \mid Wc \mid coW \mid Woc$$

$$c:: = \quad \text{concordable character}$$

$$o:: = \quad \text{optionally concordable character.} \quad \square$$

This is a recursive definition that says that a word is either a single concordable character, or a concordable character followed by a word or ... or a word followed by an optionally concordable and a concordable character. This definition can be implemented by the following algorithm.

2.2.5 Algorithm

> **Start**; word identification
> Initialise word buffer and input stream
> **Do - while** (next character not concordable)
> > Get next character
> **End - do**
> Add character to buffer, end-of-word := **false**
> **Do - while** (more characters and not end-of-word)
> > Get next character
> > **If** (concordable) **then** add to buffer
> > **Else if** (non-concordable) **then** end-of-word := **true**
> > **Else** (optionally concordable)
> > **Do** ; Get next character
> > > **If** (concordable) **then** add last two characters to buffer
> > > **Else** end-of-word := **true**
> > **End - do**
> **End - do**
> Close word buffer and input stream
> **Stop.** $\square$

The definition of section 2.2.2 removes many of the restrictions on special characters that are inherent in the original definition of section 2.2.1. However, the problems of dealing with related words still remains. Both definitions are still too general in that they regard each word as independent of all the other words. Though this may be valid for some types of text it is clearly not a good model for natural language text. In this case the lexical analyser must not only split the text into its component words but must also identify the individual word stems.

In English, and many other languages, different grammatical forms of a word are often by different suffixes. For example it is easy to identify the suffix LY in the word COMPLETELY and obtain the word stem COMPLETE. This simple approach, however, cannot cope with words such as FULLY and FLY. It is the job of a stemming algorithm to strip off these suffixes and identify the basic word stem. Such algorithms are usually based on a dictionary of valid word stems and suffixes, as in the following example.

2.2.6 Algorithm

Start; suffix removal

Get input word $w_1 w_2 \ldots w_m$
max-score = 0; best stem = ' '

For-all (stem $s_1 s_2 \ldots s_n$)

Get value k such that

$$w_i = s_i \text{ for } i = 1, 2, \ldots k, \text{ and } w_{k+1} \neq s_{k+1}$$

Set STEM_HEAD $= s_1 s_2 \ldots s_k$
     STEM_TAIL $= s_{k+1} \ldots s_n$
     SUFFIX_HEAD $= w_{k+1}$
     SHORT_SUFFIX $= w_{k+2} \ldots w_m$
     LONG_SUFFIX $= w_{k+1} \ldots w_m$

Score match of stem with word according to Fig. 2.1.
(Note 'O.K.' means that the stem or suffix is in the relevant dictionary).

If (score $>$ max-score) **then** max-score = score
                                   best-stem = stem

End- for
Return (best-stem)
Stop. □

STEM_HEAD	O.K.	O.K.	O.K.	O.K.	O.K.	O.K.	O.K.
STEM_TAIL	null	null	null	null	E	E	Y
SUFFIX_HEAD	vowel	consonant	vowel	consonant	vowel	consonant	I
SHORT_SUFFIX	–	–	O.K.	O.K.	O.K.	O.K.	O.K.
LONG_SUFFIX	O.K.	O.K.	–	–	–	–	–
SCORE	4	7	3	6	5	2	1

Fig. 2.1 – Table of suffix scores.

2.2.7 Example

Let us suppose that we have a stem dictionary which contains the stems STRIP and STRIPE, and a suffix dictionary which contains the suffixes D and ED. Then the analysis if the two words STRIPED and STRIPPED would proceed as follows:

Word	STRIPED		STRIPPED	
Possible stem	STRIP	STRIPE	STRIP	STRIPE
Stem-tail	null	null	null	E
Suffix-head	E	D	P	P
Short-suffix	D	null	ED	ED
Long-suffix	ED	D	PED	PED
Score	4	7	6	2

Thus the correct stem for STRIPED is STRIPE while the correct stem for STRIPPED is STRIP. □

This algorithm can obviously be extended to cope with other variations of English word endings and similar algorithms could be developed for other languages. For more details of these algorithms see Salton (1968). The identification of the word type (noun, adjective, adverb etc.) that is implicit in this type of algorithm is the first step in the syntactic analysis.

2.3 SYNTACTIC ANALYSIS

Once the lexical analysis has identified the individual words of a text it is the job of the syntactic analyser to extract the implicit relations between these words. The simplest type of relation is that of relative position or collocation, which can be used to distinguish word sequences such as

"blind Venetian" and "Venetian blind"

However, the important point in this example is that it is the relative positions of the words that indicates their different roles or relations; in one case "blind" is an adjective qualifying the (proper) noun "Venetian", in the other case it is a noun qualified by the adjective Venetian. The remainder of this section will be devoted to describing methods of identifying these relations.

The basic syntactic rules governing the relationships of individual words in forming a valid phrase or sentence can be stated in BNF (as were the lexical rules defined in section 2.2.4).

2.3.1 Example

We can define a class, S, of valid sentences on a vocabulary of four words a, b, c, d by

$$S:: \quad a \mid b \ T \ T \ d$$
$$T:: \quad b \ c \mid a$$

This grammar has one type of phrase, T, and five valid sentences

a, bbcbcd, bbcad, babcd, baad

The relationship in, say, babcd, can be represented as in Fig. 2.2.

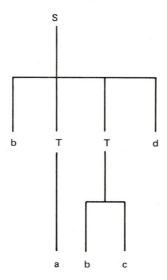

Fig. 2.2 – Phrase Structure.

or more compactly

$$(b(a)_T \ (bc)_T \ d)_S \quad \square$$

It is possible to construct a number of algorithms to identify these relations. An example of such an algorithm is given below.

2.3.2 Algorithm

Start ; Parse grammar 2.3.1

Function   PARSE_T (STRING, PARSE, REMAINDER);

given a string of characters this function attempts to identify an occurrence of T in the left most characters. The function returns the value **true** or

false depending on whether or not the parse was successful. If successful PARSE contains the occurrence of T and REMAINDER the remainder the input string.

Case (1st character = 'a');   PARST_T = **true**
                                         PARSE = $(a)_T$
                                         REMAINDER = characters 2, 3, . . .

(1st two characters = 'bc');   PARST_T = **true**
                               PARSE = $(bc)_T$
                               REMAINDER = characters 3, 4, . . .

          else   PARST_T = false
                                        PARSE = null
                                        REMAINDER = STRING

Return;

End   PARSE–T;

Function PARSE_S (STRING,PARSE)

Case   (STRING = 'a');   PARSE_S = **true**

                                     PARSE = $(a)_T$;

(character 1) = 'b' ;

& (PARST_T (character 2, 3, 4, . . .), T1, R1) = **true**

& PARST_T (R1, T2, R2) = **true**
& R2 = 'd')

                                     PARST_S = **true**
                                     PARSE = $(b\ T1\ T2\ d)_S$

          else   PARSE_S = **false**
                                     PARSE = **null**

End   PARSE_S

PARSE_S (STRING,PARSE)

Stop. □

This algorithm is a simple example of the class of parsing algorithms known collectively as top down left to right (TDLR). This describes the method in which the parsing is performed, that is, we start at the top with the sentence element and work our way down trying to parse the given string from left to right. Similar designs for bottom up and right to left parses are described by Aho and Ullman (1973).

The algorithm of section 2.3.2 is very straightforward because there is no possible ambiguity in the original grammar. If, however, we extended the second rule to

$$T:: = bc \mid a \mid ad$$

then the string

baad

could be parsed successfully as

$$(b(a)_T(a)_T d)_T$$

or unsuccessfully as

$$(b(a)_T (ad)_T$$

Thus in general it is necessary for the parse function to consider all possible parses.

So given a general BNF rule, say

$$T:: = A_1 A_2 \ldots A_n \mid B_1 B_2 \ldots B_m \mid \ldots$$

we can define a function PARSE_T which will take a given character string and return the number of possible passes of it together with details of each parse. The outline of such an algorithm is given below.

2.3.3 Algorithm

Function PARSE_T (STRING, PARSE, REMAINDER);

> This function returns an array of possible parses of the input string.

PARSE_T = 0

For $I_1 = 1$ to PARSE_A_1 (STRING, PARSE$_1$, REM$_1$)

> **For** $I_2 = 1$ to PARSE_A_2 (REM$_1$ (I$_1$), PARSE$_2$, REM$_2$)
>
> .
> .
> .
>
> **For** $I_n = 1$ to PARSE_A_n (REM$_{n-1}$ (I$_{n-1}$), PARSE$_n$, REM$_n$)
>
> PARSE_T = PARST_T + 1
>
> PARSE (PARST_T) = PARSE$_1$ (I$_1$) ... PARSE$_n$ (I$_n$))$_T$
>
> REMAINDER (PARST_T) = REM$_n$ (I$_n$)

For $J_1 = 1$ to PARSE_B_1 (. . . .   )

> .
> .
> .

END   PARST_T □

To use this, or a similar, algorithm to perform syntactic analysis it is necessary to formalise the grammatical relationships between words. A simple definition of a basic grammar is as follows:

2.3.4 Definition

$$S:: \;\; = N_p \; V_p$$
$$V_p:: \; = V \;\; N_p$$
$$N_p:: \; = A_r \; N \; | \; A_r \; A_d \; N \; | \; N$$

where the abbreviations denote the following parts of speech:

$$
\begin{array}{lll}
S & - & \text{sentence} \\
N_p & - & \text{noun phrase} \\
V_p & - & \text{verb phrase} \\
A_r & - & \text{article} \\
A_d & - & \text{adjective} \\
N & - & \text{noun} \;\square
\end{array}
$$

Using the algorithm of section 2.3.3 it is possible to construct a program to perform simple syntactic analysis. Such a program would, for example, analyse the text string:

Frobisher is a young squirrel

as

$$(((\text{Frobisher})_N)_{Np} \; ((\text{is})_V \; ((\text{a})_{Ar} \; (\text{young})_{Ad} \; (\text{squirrel})_N)_{Np})_{Vp})_S$$

This grammar can be used successfully to analyse almost all simple straightforward sentences. By adding more rules to the definition of section 2.3.4, it is possible to increase the scope of the analysis, but the system still remains too rigid to handle the full variety of natural language text. This problem has been overcome, to some extent, by the use of the basic concept of Transformational Grammar, namely that complex sentences should be regarded as transformations of basic sentences. The development of this theory and the related algorithms are outside the scope of this book, and the interested reader is referred to Chomsky (1964).

2.4 SEMANTIC ANALYSIS

The previous types of analysis that we have considered have identified the occurrence of words, or word stems, and simple relationships between those words. A semantic analysis attempts to relate this information to the user's view of the text and so facilitate the extraction of useful data. This type of analysis requires some sort of model of the data; the simplest type of model that we shall consider is the thesaurus.

A basic thesaurus is intended to give a classification of all objects that may be represented in the source text. An example of the first few categories of such a thesaurus is given below.

2.4.1 Example

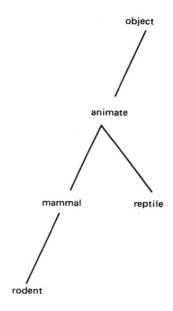

Fig. 2.3 – Semantic categories.

So in the example in Fig. 2.3, the word "squirrel" belongs to the category "rodent" and so also to "mammal", but not to "reptile". In general, each node in such a tree will correspond not to a single word but to a group of synonymous words. This leads to the following definitions:

2.4.2 Definition

A synonym ring is a set of words or phrases (which are regarded as synonymous).

A thesaurus is a set of trees whose nodes are synonym rings. (The parent-child relation is renamed the broader–narrower term relation, for example the broader term for 'animate' is 'object' and its narrower terms are 'mammal' and 'reptile'.

A thesaurus is labelled if each node has a unique label. (This is called the preferred term of the synonym ring). □

An example of part of a labelled thesaurus is given below.

2.4.3 Example

321 : Sun, Solar

    321.16 : Solar energy, alternative energy

       321.16.2 : Solar power plants

    . . . .

352 : wind, air, draught

    352.16 : wind energy, alternative energy

    . . . .

589 : Bibliography, Information Services

    589.1 : Information Storage and Retrieval Systems, Data Processing

       589.1.1 : Database management

       589.1.2 : Information networks

    . . . . □

The first stage of the semantic analysis is to identify the preferred terms for all the words occurring in the text. This is normally a simple table look-up, the problems caused in the case of ambiguous words (that is, words occurring in more than one synonym ring) are discussed by Earl (1972).

The original words in the parsed output of the lexical analysis can then be replaced by their corresponding preferred terms, thus giving a standard representation of the text. We shall see later how this can be used to extract information from the text.

The construction of such a thesaurus is invariably a manual operation. There are, however, three simple rules:

(i) high frequency words are likely to be fairly general and should occur towards the root of the trees,

(ii) low frequency words are likely to be fairly specific and should occur towards the leaves of the trees,

(iii) words which frequently occur together are likely to be fairly similar and should occur in the same area of the tree.

It is possible to construct automatically word lists which are based on frequency of occurrence and co-occurrence of words, and such lists can form a useful starting point for the construction of a thesaurus. Further information on this subject can be found in Freeman (1976).

A related type of semantic analysis is based on the notion of **semantic categories**. A semantic category is a representation of one of a number of basic attributes which can be used to express the meaning of a word. Thus the first two levels of the thesaurus of section 2.4.1 correspond to the semantic categories 'physical object' and 'animate' and all the nodes lower down in the tree inherit the semantic categories of their parent nodes. Such categories will either be present or absent in any description; there are other categories such as 'colour' or 'height' will also have an associated qualifier, either descriptive or numeric.

Thus the word 'strawberry' is represented by the categories:

'physical object', 'colour (red)', etc.

This is essentially a dictionary definition, with the important difference that the words used in the definition are taken from a small well-defined set. This type of representation depends on building up a complete list of categories so that any word can be represented by a set of these categories.

Like a thesaurus, however, this set of categories has to be developed manually. More details and applications of this type of analysis can be found in Teskey (1978).

2.5 NUMERICAL ANALYSIS OF TEXT

The previous sections have been concerned with analysing text into its component lexical syntactic and semantic tokens. The analysis can, however, be extended to include the mathematical, and in particular the statistical, properties of these tokens. The basic tool in this type of analysis is to measure the frequency of occurrence of text fragments — parts of words, individual words, or phrases.

2.5.1 Definition
Given a fixed set of text fragments

$$V = \{W_1, W_2, \ldots W_n\}$$

(where W_1, W_2 etc. are parts of words, individual words, or phrases then the vector representation of a text document D is

$$D_V = (f_1, f_2, \ldots f_n)$$

where f_i is the frequency of occurrence of W_i in D. □

2.5.2 Example
If $V = \{$ all, rodents, mammals, animals, objects$\}$ then the vector representation of the text

D : All rodents are mammals and all mammals are animals

is $D_V = \{2, 1, 2, 1, 0\}$ □

It is customary to extend the above definition to allow the vocabulary V to contain preferred terms from a thesaurus and to accumulate all occurrences of synonyms and their preferred terms. The most important case of this is where the vocabulary V is precisely the set of preferred terms. In cases such as these where the vector V is very large, much of D_V will be zero and it is customary to represent just the non-zero elements together with their associated co-ordinate. This is illustrated in the following example.

2.5.3 Example

Using the thesaurus of section 2.4.3 the text

> D : "There is a growing need for a central bibliography on solar energy and the proposed information service would meet this need"

is represented by

$$D_v = (2(589), 1(321.16), \ldots)$$

that is, two occurrences of 589 : Bibliography, one occurrence of 321.16 ... □

This type of numerical representation takes account of simple word frequencies but not the order and relation in which these words occur. It is possible to extend the representation to include the frequency of occurrence of word pairs, triples, etc. In this way we can generate new text fragments corresponding to the high frequency pairs and triples; such fragments are called statistical phrases.

A more detailed numerical representation can be developed from the 'semantic category' representation. In the simplest case if we have a set of categories

$$C = \{C_1, C_2, \ldots C_m\}$$

then each word can be represented by the subset of those categories to which it belongs. In general, however, the inclusion of a word in a given category will be a probabilistic or fuzzy decision rather than an absolute one. For example, under 'human' there may be three categories 'baby', 'child' and 'adult'; it is clear that a ten year old would be a child, while a ten month old would be a baby. What is not clear is whether a two year old is a baby or a child. The theory of fuzzy sets (Zadeh 1965) allows an entity to have a degree of membership of a set; in this case the two year old might belong 50% to the category of 'baby' and 50% to the category of 'child'; as he grew older the degree of membership would change. So it is more appropriate to represent the word as a vector

$$W = (p_1, p_2, \ldots p_m)$$

where p_i is the degree of (fuzzy) membership of W in the category C_i. Text can then be presented by a sequence of these vectors, see Teskey (1978).

2.6 ALGORITHMIC ANALYSIS OF TEXT

The types of analysis discussed in the preceding section do not go very far towards codifying the meaning of text documents. In many cases this is not required, or even possible in the present state of the art. At present such detailed analysis has succeeded only in very well-defined areas of discourse (Winograd

1972). An alternative approach is to recognise that in certain fields the standard textual analysis methods will not be sufficiently powerful and that effort is better devoted to developing algorithmic representation which can be handled more easily. In its simplest form this method can be applied to text which describes a process, and it consists of analysing the textual description to produce an algorithmic description. The analysis is performed manually and the most important feature of this approach lies in the language used for the algorithmic description. Examples of such languages can be found in Stamper (1976).

2.7 SUMMARY

In this chapter we have described a number of ways of analysing textual material. The results of these various types of analysis range from the identification of individual lexical tokens to a formal knowledge representation language. In general the simpler methods have a very wide range of applications while the more powerful types of analysis have to be specially tailored to a particular environment. Though the latter type of system has been developed for a number of diverse applications, there is, as yet, no forseeable way of constructing a universal analyser of this complexity and power. So in any information system it is necessary to match the type of linguistic analysis to the users requirements and to the type of storage and retrieval methods used. Some of these methods are described in the following chapters.

3

Data Storage

A man should keep his little brain attic stocked with all the furntirue that he is likely to use, and the rest he can put away in the lumber room of his library where he can get at it if he wants.

Sir Arthur Conan Doyle
The Five Orange Pips

3.1 REQUIREMENTS FOR DATA STORAGE

Once a piece of text has been analysed by one of the methods outlined in the previous chapter, it is necessary to store the result of that analysis, and possibly the original source text. The data should be stored in an efficient structure to reduce the amount of work needed to extract any required data. The structures used for storing the source text will depend on the type of text and also the user's requirements; the storage of the analysed text will also depend on these features as well as on the type of analysis used. The storage system must make it possible to extract any data from the analysed text and to retrieve the source text corresponding to this data. There should also be facilities to alter the source text and to make corresponding alterations to the analysed data.

In any system for storing and retrieving textual material there will be three ways of looking at the structure of the stored text. They are:

   (i) user view
  (ii) system view
 (iii) physical view.

The user view shows how the data base appears to the user and should correspond to his information requirements, the system view shows how the data base is implemented and maintained, while the physical view shows how the text is stored in a particular physical device. These three levels can be seen, not only in computer systems, but also in manual ones. So, for example, a library subject catalogue can be regarded as:

    (i) a sequence of bibliographic records ordered according to a standard subject classification — the user view

   (ii) a set of working procedures to be used by library staff for cataloguing new material as it arrives in the library — the system view

  (iii) a set of typed cards stored in a cabinet — the physical view.

The important point is that these three views should be independent, internal changes at one level should not affect other levels. For example, the use of larger card cabinets should not affect the user view of the system. There will, necessarily, be some dependence between these views which reflects the implicit structure of the data base, but this should be kept to a minimum. In particular, the physical view should have little or no impact on the user view — this allows changes to be made to the computer hardware without affecting the user. For most of this chapter we will concentrate on the user and system views of data storage.

3.2 STORAGE OF SOURCE TEXT

In Chapter 2 the source text was initially regarded as a sequence of characters. It would be possible to store the text in this form as a single sequential file. This, however, would make the retrieval and updating of the source text a lengthy process, so it is desirable to use a limited amount of analysis to structure the text into a form more suitable for storage. The most common method involves splitting the text into manageable units; these units are referred to as **records** or **documents**. There are three main methods of storing such documents, (omitting for the moment content addressable memories and other special hardware).

    (i) indexed sequential

   (ii) hierarchical

  (iii) clustered

The advantages and disadvantages of these are outlined below.

3.2.1 Definition

An indexed sequential text file stores text as an ordered sequence of records and maintains a primary index to selected records in the sequence. □

3.2.2 Example

If each text record is given a unique two level reference number then a possible indexed sequential file structure is illustrated in Fig. 3.1. □

Obviously by varying the size of the index it is possible to vary the structure from a simple sequential file to a fully indexed file. The method can provide rapid access to specified records and easy addition, deletion and modification of records. It may not, however, accurately represent the implicit structure of

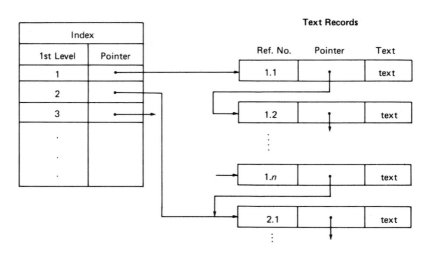

Fig. 3.1 — Indexed sequential file structure.

the data relating to an imprecise user request. In many cases imposing such a strict order on the data means that implicitly related text records are not directly linked. For example, it is difficult to arrange the text of a legal document with head-notes, foot-notes and side-notes as a simple sequential character string, in such cases a hierarchical storage system is more appropriate.

3.2.3 Definition
A hierarchical text file stores text as a set of records with pointers forming a tree structure. □

3.2.4 Example
The full text of an Act of Parliament could be stored in a hierarchical text file as shown in Fig. 3.2. □

   This type of structure is very general — the 'List of Sections' with pointers to individual sections is obviously very similar to the indexed sequential structure defined in section 3.2.1. It solves many of the problems of browsing through the text to locate related documents; though as the number of documents increases it will take the user considerably longer to browse to records at the bottom of the tree. It is also important to note that the simple hierarchical approach does not permit any record to be related to more than one parent record; to overcome this restriction more general networks must be used (Date 1975). It is obviously easy to add and modify records. However, some care is needed in deleting records, to ensure that the dependent records are not left detached from the rest of the tree.

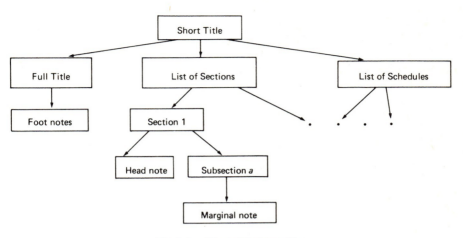

Fig. 3.2 – Hierarchical text file.

3.2.5 Definition
A clustered text file stores text as sets (or clusters) of documents according to some specified criterion of similarity between documents. The most commonly used criterion is that documents are in the same cluster if they have a high similarity coefficient, where a similarity coefficient is formally defined below. □

3.2.6 Example
Acts of Parliament, as published by HMSO, contain references or citations to other acts. If one act cites another, this implies a semantic relation between the two acts; the more often the act is cited the stronger is the relationship between

Pensioners' Payments and National Insurance Act 1973, c. 61 . . . . } 0.891
Pensioners' Payments Act 1974, c. 54 . . . . }

Export Guarantees Amendment Act 1975, c. 19 . . . . } 0.455
Export Guarantees Act 1975, c. 38. . . . . }

Representation of the People Act 1974, c.10 . . . . } 0.444
Representation of the People (No. 2) Act 1974, c. 13. . . . . }

Finance Act 1974, c. 30 . . . . } 0.708
Finance (No. 2) Act 1975, c. 45. . . . . }   } 0.622   } 0.433
Finance Act 1973, c. 51 . . . . }
Finance Act 1975, c. 7. . . . . }

The figures show the similarity coefficient for each cluster.

Fig. 3.3 – Clustering of legal texts.

the two. In a recent study, Anderson (1976) used the pattern of citations of Acts of Parliament to measure the similarity between acts. Part of the resulting clustered file is shown in Fig. 3.3. These groupings are obvious but the technique does produce some non-obvious clusters; these may well show changes in the substance of the law and indicate new subject areas being developed. □

3.2.7 Definition
A similarity coefficient, s, on a set of records R is a function $s : R \times R \to [0, 1]$ such that

(i) $s(r, r) = 1$
(ii) $s(p, q) = s(q, p)$ □

3.2.8 Example
Given a set of documents

$$D = \{d_1, d_2, \ldots d_m\}$$

consisting of text drawn from a vocabulary

$$V = \{W_1, W_2, \ldots W_x\}$$

let f_{ij} = frequency of word W_i in document d_j.
Then $s : D \times D \to [0, 1]$

by $(d_i, d_j) \longrightarrow \dfrac{(\Sigma f_{ki} \, f_{kj})}{\Sigma f_{ki}^2 \; \Sigma f_{kj}^2}$

where the summations are for $k = 1$ to n defines a similarity coefficient on D.

    The proof is trivial — s measures the cosine of the angle between the vector representations of elements of D. This is one of the standard similarity coefficients used in text processing; details of it and other coefficients can be found in Salton (1975). □
To make use of results from Metric Spaces, as in the theorem of section 3.2.10 it is often easier to deal with a dissimilarity coefficient and so we define

$$d = 1 - s$$

We can now define a whole hierarchy of clusters, starting at level 0 with the individual documents and combing two clusters at level h if and only if there is an element, a, in the first and b, in the second cluster such that

$$d(a, b) = h$$

This gives rise to a dendogram or tree diagram such as the one shown in Fig. 3.4.

3.2.9 Example
In the dendogram in Fig. 3.4 $d(a, b) = 0.1$ and so a and b form a cluster at level 0.1. Similarly one of the elements of the cluster $\{a, b, c\}$ is a distance 0.4 from an

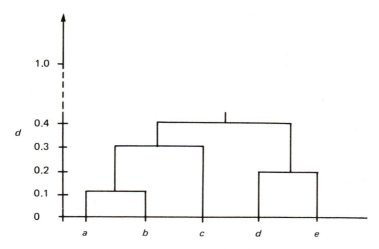

Fig. 3.4 – Sample dendogram.

element in the cluster $\{d, e\}$ and so these two clusters combine to form a single cluster at level 0.4. □

The following formal definition and theorem have been included for completeness, and may be omitted by non-mathematical readers.

3.2.10 Definition

A dendogram on a set of records, R, is a function $c : [0, 1] \rightarrow R'$ where R' is the set of all partitions of R and

     (i) if $i \leqslant j$ then $c(i) \leqslant i(j)$
     (ii) $c(1) = R$ □

3.2.11 Theorem

If d is a dissimilarity coefficient on R and $\mathbf{U}$ is the set of all dissimilarity coefficients which satisfy the additional condition

$$U(p, r) \leqslant \max (U(p, q),\ U(q, r))$$

then $d' = \max \{U \in \mathbf{U} : U \leqslant d\}$

defines a dendogram d'' on R by

$$d''(h) = \{(p, q) : d'(p, q) \leqslant h\}$$

The proof involves showing that d'' is an equivalence relation and hence a partition on R, it is then trivial to show that it satisfies the conditions of the definition in section 3.2.10. Details of the proof can be found Jardine and Sibson (1971). This type of dendogram is known as the single link cluster and can be built using the following algorithm. □

3.2.12 Algorithm

Start ; single link cluster
Set up cluster containing first element

Do-while (more elements)
        Get next element n, and find nearest element m
        Add n to all clusters above level $d(m, n)$ containing m.
        Form a cluster at level $d(m, n)$ contianing n and largest cluster
        below level $d(m, n)$ which contains m.

End-do

Stop □

This algorithm obviously allows for the addition of new records by repeating the statements within the DO loop. Deleting and modifying records, however, is slightly more difficult. For more details of this method and its application to legal text see Boreham and Niblett (1976).

In any text processing system one must decide which method of storage to use. The choice will obviously depend on the type of material to be stored; for highly structured text then the hierarchical storage might be preferred while for general free text a clustered file may be more appropriate. The user requirement, however, is even more important. If it is anticipated that the user will have a very good idea of what data he will require, then the indexed sequential structure would be the most efficient. For example, in a system dealing with correspondence where letters are referred to by the date they were written, these letters could be stored in chronological order in an indexed sequential file with an index to the first letter written each day. A clustered file allows a certain amount of browsing through the text in each cluster, and reference has already been made to the application of this to legal text. Finally the hierarchical structure provides a very good method for leading naive users through the text by means of simple choices at each node of the tree. This is perhaps best illustrated by Prestel and similar systems, where the text is stored in the leaves of a large tree and the internal nodes contain indices and pointers to the data lower down the tree.

3.3 COMPRESSION OF TEXT

The previous section discussed various structures for storing text records, as distinct from methods of storing the text in records themselves. It has been assumed that the text is regarded as a sequence of characters and that each character is stored in the computer as a fixed binary code. It is worth pointing out that this system may be inefficient especially on computer systems employing a standard 8-bit character code. This type of code can represent 256 different characters but in general text requires no more than 80 different characters (upper and lower case letters, digits and puctuation marks) and so over 170 character codes are unused. One can devise coding methods whereby frequently occurring sequences of characters are given one of these unused codes. (see, for example Maggs 1974). This can be extended to use a much larger number of frequently occurring character strings with a corresponding increase in efficiency. In these cases it is customary to construct a dictionary of these character strings using a sample of the text to be stored in the system. If we assume that such a sample has been analysed to provide the frequency of occurrence of each possible character string then the following algorithm will produce a set of character strings (n-grams) for text compression. The algorithm requires a threshold frequency F and a maximum n-gram length N. These parameters can be adjusted by trial and error to give the required number of n-grams.

3.3.1 Algorithm

> **Start** ; n-gram generation
> Get frequency of all l-grams (single characters)
> Select l-grams with frequency $< F$
>
> **Do** $n = 2$ **to** N
>> Get frequency of all n-grams which start with any of the remaining (n-1) grams.
>> From these select those n-grams with frequency $< F$
>
> **End-do**
>
> **Stop** □

Having constructed such a dictionary of n-grams it is then possible to assign a code to each n-gram and encode the text using the following algorithm.

3.3.2 Algorithm

> **Start** ; text compression
> Set pointer to first CHAR of input text
> Set $I = 1$, CODE = CHAR, LENGTH = 1
>
> **Do-while** (more text)
>
> **Do-while** (there is an n-gram beginning with the first I characters after the pointer)
>> **If** (complete match) **then** save code in CODE and length in LENGTH
>> $I = I + 1$
>
> **End-do**
> Output CODE, advance pointer by LENGTH
>
> **End-do**
>
> **Stop** □

3.3.3 Example

If we assume a threshold frequency of 2 and an n-gram length of 3 then algorithm of section 3.3.1 applied to

IF ∧ WE ∧ TAKE ∧ THIS ∧ SENTENCE ∧ .

will yield the following 1, 2 and 3-grams.

1	A	8	IF	20	E∧T
2	C	9	IS	21	E∧.
3	F	10	NT	22	ENT
4	H	11	NC	23	ENC
5	K	12	S∧	24	∧TA
6	W	13	SE	25	∧TH
7	.	14	TA		
		15	TE		
		16	TH		
		17	∧W		
		18	∧S		
		19	∧.		

where ∧ denotes the space character.

Then using algorithm of section 3.3.2 to code the above sentence gives

8, 17, 20, 1, 5, 20, 4, 9, 18, 22, 23, 21

The conventional storage of the original text would require 26 8-bit bytes, that is, 208 bits the coded form could be stored in 12 5-bit bytes, that is, 60 bits. It is a simple matter to decode this version using table look-up techniques. □

This compression has the effect of storing and transporting the text more efficiently but it should have no impact on the logic of the text processing system. It has been suggested by Adamson and Boreham (1974) that these n-grams should form the basis of the text analysis. It is outside the scope of this book to dicuss this and so we shall maintain our original assumption that the character is the basic unit of text, with the understanding that at the lowest level there may be a system of text compression and decompression on input and output.

3.4 DICTIONARY STRUCTURES

Just as the analysis of text is based on the identification of individual words so the storage of analysed text is also based on the word. The storage system is usually centred around a dictionary structure that contains a list of every word identified in the text together with pointers to the information stored about that word. This is illustrated in Fig. 3.5.

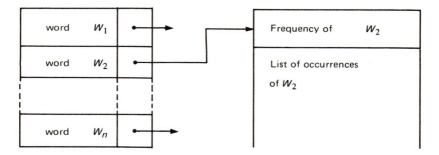

Fig. 3.5 – Dictionary structures.

The words in this structure could equally well be word-stems, phrases or thesaurus entries such as preferred terms. The major problem is in storing the structure in such a way as to allow efficient retrieval and updating of individual words.

The sequential and hierarchical files that were discussed in section 3.2 can also be used to store a dictionary. There are two additional types of structure we shall consider: distributed or multi-way trees and scatter or hash storage.

3.4.1 Definition
A multi-way tree is a tree in which each node can have a number of pointers and each pointer is indexed by a character from the standard character set. A terminal node represents the word formed by the characters on the path between the root and the node. □

3.4.2 Example
In Fig. 3.6 the symbol ϕ represents the terminator and the two terminal nodes represent the words AN and AND as shown. This structure can be represented by a 2-dimensional array as in Fig. 3.7. Each column corresponds to a node in the multi-way tree, together with its corresponding pointers. □

This type of structure is intrinsically very fast; however, it does require a large amount of storage space. We shall see in the algorithm of section 3.4.6 how this problem can be overcome.

3.4.3 Definition
A hashing system consists of

- (i) a function which maps arbitrary character strings onto a fixed range (1 to N) of positive integers, and
- (ii) an algorithm which can be used to adjust the above function to ensure that it is 1-1 on any set of N character strings. □

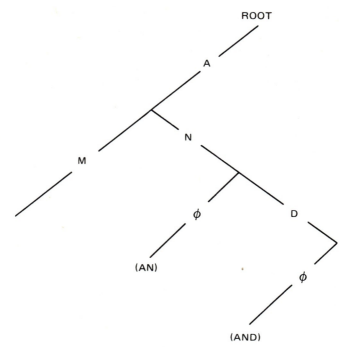

Fig. 3.6 — Multi-way tree.

	1	2	3	4
A	2			
· · ·				
D			4	
· · ·				
N		3		
· · ·				
φ			↓ (AN)	↓ (AND)

Fig. 3.7 — Representation of a multi-way tree.

3.4.4 Example

If $c = c_1 c_2 \ldots c_n$ is a character string of length n, then we may assume that each c_i is an integer – namely the corresponding character code. Let $h(c) = \Sigma\ i\ c_i$ modulo $(1021) + 1$ then h satisfies the first part of the definition of section 3.4.3. Further if c is one of a sequence of character strings then let M be the least non-negative integer such that h' is unique, where

$$h'(c) = h(c) - M\,(h(c) \bmod (1019) + 1)$$

that is $h'(c) \neq h'(c')$ for any c' earlier in the sequence of character strings. This defines an algorithm which satisfies the second part of the definition of section 3.4.3. The proof is left as an exercise for the reader – details can be found in Severance and Duhne (1976). The method can be implemented in the following algorithm. □

3.4.5 Algorithm

　　Start ; hash storage
　　Get next character string $c = c_1 c_2 \ldots c_n$
　　Set $h = \Sigma i c_i$ modulo $(1021) + 1$

　　If (entry h in hash table is empty)

　　　　Then store c in position h

　　　　Else set $k = h$ modulo $(1019) + 1$

　　　　　　Do-while (entry h is not empty) set $h = h - k$;
　　　　　　Store c in position h

　　Stop. □

This is only a very brief outline of some possible dictionary structures; for a more comprehensive introduction the reader is referred to Knuth (1973).

In any given application the choice of dictionary structure will depend very much on the type of text to be stored. Thus a bibliographic data base may contain a series of unique accession numbers and these could best be stored in an ordered list. In a chemical data base there may be no requirement to produce alphabetical lists of chemical names and so a hash table would be appropriate. English language text, is perhaps the most difficult since there is such a variety of word forms and lengths (Coleman 1976). One possibility is to use a compound system of multi-way tree to index on the first few characters and then store the remaining parts of the words in ordered lists. This makes use of the efficiency of the multi-way tree in the initial part of the dictionary structure without incurring its overheads throughout the whole structure. It is illustrated in Fig. 3.8 which shows how the words

　　　　CAT, CATCH, CATTLE, COMPARE, COUNT, COUNTER

and pointers to their reference are stored. New words can be added to this structure using the algorithm of section 3.4.6.

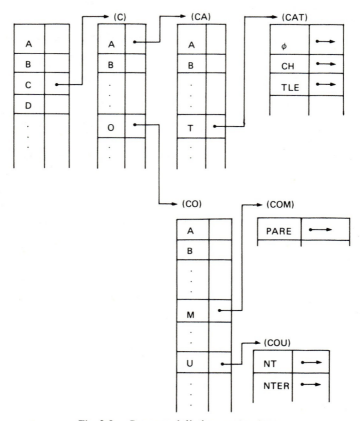

Fig. 3.8 – Compound dictionary structure.

3.4.6 Algorithm

Start ; dictionary structure
Get new word
Set current node = root

Do I = 1 to 2
    Set c = character I
    Get pointer at position c in current node

    If (null) **Then** Link in new mode
                      Set current node = new node

          Else   Set current node = indicated node
End-do

Set c = character 3
Get pointer at position c is current node

If (null) **Then** Link in word list
Search list for word

If (found) **Then** Add reference to reference list

              Else   Add in new word
                     Link in new reference list
Stop. □

3.5 CONTENT ADDRESSABLE MEMORIES

In the previous section we discussed various solutions to the problem of constructing suitable dictionary structures to store and retrieve individual words and their associated reference lists. All the methods considered so far have been based on a conventional von Neumann type computer. Recently there have been considerable developments in the design and construction of special purpose computer hardware and in particular content addressable memories (Thurber and Wald 1975).

The development of content addressable memories promises to provide an ideal solution to the problem of dictionary structures, and possibly to other problems in the field of text processing. The dictionary structure defined by the algorithm of section 3.4.6 can be represented conceptually as a file of records of the form

        word ; pointer to reference

To access this record it is necessary to perform a software search through the dictionary looking for the required word and then get the pointer to the corresponding reference list. In a content addressed memory the records are accessed not by physical location but by content. Thus the hardware searches through the memory looking for the required word and outputs the record containing the word and its associated reference pointer. The advantage of this is that the search is performed much more efficiently by hardware than would be possible using conventional software.

The basic structure of a CAM can be represented as in Fig. 3.9.

The data is stored in a number of records in the main part of the memory. To search the memory for a given word, the required word is set up in the relevant position in the Interrogate Register and the remainder of the record is masked out using the Mask Register. The hardware then interrogates all the records in parallel, or at least all those records with the correct control bits set in the mark register. A flag is set in the Mark Register for those records that satisfied the search request; these records can then be output for further processing. More details of the operation of CAMs can be found in Lea (1977).

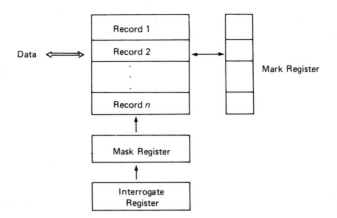

Fig. 3.9 – Basic CAM structure.

3.6 KNOWLEDGE STRUCTURES

The syntactic analysis and semantic analysis discussed in Chapter 2 attempt to go beyond the simple identification of words to try and extract some form of the meaning of the text. The results of this type of analysis will obviously require a more complex form of storage than those we have looked at so far. The basic requirement is that the storage system should contain, either explicitly or implicitly, a model of the universe to which the text refers – such a model is known as a knowledge structure.

A simple but very powerful model is the relational one developed by Codd (1970). Suppose our universe of discourse is confined to information on the personnel file of a large firm, then this information could be stored in a number of relations of the form

> **Employee** (NI – number, name, date-of-birth)
>
> **Job**   (NI – number, pay, job description)
>
> etc.

Thus information such as:

> "John Smith works as a secretary"

could be stored as two triples:

> (12769, SMITH JOHN,)
>
> (12769, ,SECRETARY)

in the **Employee** and **Job** relations. This forms the basis of many data base systems; in most of these the text is input in a very formal language; this makes the analysis much simpler but the basic principal remains the same. For more information about the details of relational systems and their applications the reader is referred to Date (1975).

The relational view has proved very successful in representing well structured data, but a more powerful system is required to handle the greater generality that is implicit in natural language text. The concept of a frame has been introduced to meet this requirement.

3.6.1 Definition
A frame consists of a relational data structure together with a set of procedures for finding the data to fill each component of the relation. Note that in processing textual material, each frame will usually store an item of information about the universe of discourse; typically this will be the result of the analysis of a phrase or sentence. □

3.6.2 Example
Consider the information a travel agent would require to organise a simple journey for a client; this data could be stored in a number of frames as in Fig. 3.10.

	DATA		PROCEDURES	
	NAME	TYPE	SERVANT	DEMON
DIALOGUE	Client Topic	Person Trip	Create	Link to traveller
TRIP	Traveller When Home	Person Date City	Get date Default	
DATE	Month Day Year	Character 1 .. 31 Integer	Get month Get day Default	

Fig. 3.10 – Frame structure.

In this example there are two possible types of procedure associated with any data item: servant and demon. Servants are procedures that are executed on demand while demons are activated automatically for each data item. Thus after analysing a sentence such as:

"I want to fly to Dublin on the 17th March".

the analysed data could be stored in a series of frames as above. The 'DIALOGUE' frame creates a 'TRIP' frame and the client, I, is automatically linked to the traveller slot. The other fields are filled in similarly. For a fuller description of this example see Bobrow *et al.* (1977). □

This frame based approach is an attempt to overcome the traditional distinction between program and data. The next stage in this process is to regard objects not as frames but rather as computers which interact with other objects by sending messages between them. This is the basis of object oriented programming languages — a detailed description of these is outside the scope of this book but more details can be found in Goldstein and Bobrow (1980).

3.7 VECTOR STRUCTURES

The vector representation produced by the numerical analysis can be stored using the same techniques that are used for storing the source text. However, because of the close relation between the vector representation and the clustered file it makes sense to store these vectors in a clustered file. The representation of the vectors is still a problem. In a reasonably sized system the total vocabulary will be very large and so the vectors will be very long and require a large amount of storage space. However, the vocabulary of any one document will be small in relation to the whole vocabulary, and so most of the entries in the vector will be zero. There are two equivalent methods of storing such vectors efficiently — run-length coded and coordinate indexed.

3.7.1 Definition
The run-length coded form of a vector stores a run of n zeros as a flag followed by the integer n. □

3.7.2 Example
Since the entries in a document vector are always positive we can use the sign bit to flag a run of zeros. Thus

$$(0, 0, 0, 2, 3, 0, 10, 0, 0, 0, 5)$$

is represented as

$$(-3, 2, 3, -1, 10, -4, 5)$$ □

3.7.3 Definition
The coordinate indexed form of a vector stores the non-zero elements together with their associated coordinates. □

3.7.4 Example
The vector in the example of section 3.7.2 would be represented as two parallel arrays

$$(2, 3, 10, 5)$$
$$(4, 5, 7, 12) \quad \square$$

3.8 SUMMARY

In this chapter we have presented a number of ways of storing data, both the original source text and also the analysed text. The choice of storage system for the source text will depend on the user application and the type of text to be stored, the options considered were sequential, hierarchical and clustered files. The storage of analysed text depends much more on the type of analysis that has been performed; the results of a simple lexical analysis can be stored in a dictionary structure while a fuller semantic analysis would require a more complex knowledge structure. As with the different types of analysis, it is the simpler forms of storage that have the widest application. We shall see, however, in the following chapters that these methods can form the basis of quite powerful systems.

4

Data Extraction

Knowledge is of two kinds. We know a subject ourselves, or we know where we can find information on it.

Samuel Johnson
Boswell's *Life of Johnson*

4.1 INTRODUCTION

In the previous two chapters we have looked at various methods of analysing and storing textual materials. In this chapter we will discuss some of the ways in which useful data can be extracted from the analysed text which is held in these storage structures. There are three major facets to data extraction: function, application and implementation. The function of a data extraction system can be classified either as document retrieval or as fact retrieval. Spark Jones and Kay (1973, p. 175) distinguish these two types of system as follows:

> The document retrieval system responds to a users request for information, not by supplying the required information itself, but by providing documents, or the description of documents, in which there is some hope of finding the information. A fact retrieval system, on the other hand, aims to answer questions directly ... it must be capable of finding facts ... on the basis of which to infer a correct answer to the question.

This distinction is often reflected in the application of each of these types of system; document retrieval systems tend to be applied to bibliographic information, legal documents and free (unstructured) text in general, while fact retrieval systems tend to be applied to personnel files, stock control information and other types of structured data. In this chapter we shall concentrate on the methods used to implement such systems. Document and fact retrieval systems tend naturally to be implemented using different algorithms. However, we shall see that this distinction becomes blurred and that there is, in fact, a whole range of methods, some of which can be used for document retrieval, some for fact retrieval and some for both. We have introduced the term data extraction to cover this range of methods — it includes browsing, best-fit matching, conditional retrieval, rule following and deductive methods. These topics are discussed in the following sections.

4.2 BROWSING

When a user requests information from a data base we assume that, had he the time and stamina, he could look through all the text in the system to find the data he required. For anything other than a very small data base it is obviously impractical for the user to search through it all, but browsing through part of the text is still a valid method of extracting information. The use of browsing allows the user to see the text exactly as it is and he may find information that he would not have found using any other method. However any browsing facility has to balance two conflicting requirements:

(i) the need to limit the user's effort by directing him to areas of the text that the system thinks are likely to be relevant, and
(ii) the need to maintain the freedom of random browsing.

The three methods that are outlined each strike a different balance between these two requirements.

The main method used to implement browsing is the document pointer. Each text document will have one or more browsing pointers attached to it, when the user browses to that document he can then follow any one of the pointers to look at another document in the data base. The browsing can start either with a fixed base article in the data base or with a document retrieved using one of the methods described in the following sections. The browsing pointers can be independent of the pointers used to maintain the data structures of section 3.2, but obviously the system will be more efficient if the browsing structure corresponds to the logical data structure. In either case there are three main types of browsing:

(i) sequential
(ii) hierarchical
(iii) clustered.

The main features of these are as follows. In sequential browsing the user starts at the first document in the data base, or one of the selected documents in the index, and looks at each succeeding document in turn. This provides little direction to the user but because he can, potentially, scan the whole data base he has a better chance of fortuitous discovery of useful information. In hierachical browsing the user starts at the root of the hierarchy or tree and is guided to areas of likely interest. Each node should contain not only pointers to its dependent nodes but also some indication of the information that is stored in the sub-trees. The user can then make a choice as to which branch of the tree to follow. This limits the amount of text the user has to browse through. If the user decides that the text he is looking at is not really relevant and he wants to look at another area, then he must either back-track up the tree or else abandon his current search and start again. In some applications this may cause problems. The clustered file attempts to provide the best of both these methods — the system gathers together all the documents it thinks are related and the user is then free to browse round each cluster sequentially or jump to another cluster.

One type of browsing we have not yet considered is that provided by the Spatial Data Management System (Bolt 1979). This is based on the observation that we often refer to documents by their physical description and location. For example, I know that certain conference proceedings are in a red box file on the bottom of my bookcase and if I wanted to direct anybody to information in those proceedings that is what I would tell them. Similarly, books in a library can often be found more quickly using a rough idea of location, colour and size than by the conventional catalogue. The Spatial Data Management system sttempts to take advantage of this fluency with descriptions involving space, size, colour etc. Each document is represented by a picture of itself at a particular location in a two-dimensional 'Dataland'. An 'aerial view' of Dataland is presented to the user and he has complete freedom to browse round and home in on particular items. This system is at present in the experimental stage but it seems likely that the concept of spatial data management will prove useful in future systems.

4.3 BEST-FIT MATCHING

The next type of data extraction that we will consider is based on the notion of pattern matching. If the user can formalise his request for data simply by expressing it in natural language, then that request can be regarded as a text document just like any other document in the data base. The system can then apply some pattern matching algorithms to identify those documents that match the user's request. The hope is that by browsing through this limited set of documents the user will indeed find the data he wanted. This approach obviously depends very much on the type of pattern matching that is used and the form of the analysed text on which the matching is performed.

The most widely used methods employ a similarity coefficient acting on a vector representation of the text. Thus we shall assume that the user's question, Q, has been analysed to give

$$q = (q_1, q_2, \ldots q_n)$$

where q_i is the frequency of occurrence of word W_i in the question. Then continuing with the notation from section 3.2.7 we can calculate the similarity coefficient between q and any document d_i by

$$s(q, d_i) = \frac{(\Sigma f_{ki} q_k)^2}{\Sigma f_{ki}^2 \, \Sigma q_k^2}$$

In this coefficient the numerator can be regarded as a sum of local and global weights; the f_{ki} represent the local importance of the word W_k in a particular document d_i, while the q_k represents the global importance of the word to the whole search. The denominator can be regarded as a weighting factor to bring the coefficient into the range $(0, 1)$. Having calculated this similarity coefficient for all the documents in the data base it is then possible to rank the documents in decreasing order of similarity and present them to the user in that order. If all the documents are of a similar length and have a similar word frequency distribution then the summation Σf_{ki}^2 will be almost constant over all the documents in the data base. So in practice, we can ignore the weighting factor in the cosine similarity coefficient; generalising the numerator gives the following definition.

4.3.1 Definition
A general vector ranking system takes a question q and orders the document d_i of a data base in decreasing order of the value of the function

$$r(q, d_i) = \Sigma l_{ki} g_k$$

where l_{ki} represents the local importance of the word W_k in the document d_i and g_k represents the global importance of W_k to the search question. □

4.3.2 Example
The following are some of the possibilities for the functions l and g.

4.3.2.1 *Binary*

$$l_{ki} = \begin{array}{ll} 1 & \text{if } W_k \text{ is in } d_i \\ 0 & \text{otherwise} \end{array}$$

$$g_k = \begin{array}{ll} 1 & \text{if } W_k \text{ is in } q \\ 0 & \text{otherwise} \end{array}$$

This is the simplest type of ranking and serves as a base for comparing the other types.

4.3.2.2 *Term frequency*

$$l_{ki} = f_{ki}$$
$$g_k = \begin{array}{ll} 1 & \text{if } W_k \text{ is in } q \\ 0 & \text{otherwise.} \end{array}$$

4.3.2.3 *Inner product*

$$l_{ki} = f_{ki}$$
$$g_k = q_k$$

This is essentially the cosine similarity coefficient.

4.3.2.4 *Inverse document frequency*

$$l_{ki} = f_{ki}$$
$$g_k = 1 - \log(m_k/m) \qquad \text{if } W_k \text{ is in } q$$
$$ 0 \quad \text{otherwise}$$

where m = number of documents

m_k = number of documents containing W_k.

This function is based on the assumption that in any search we should attach a low weight to common words, such as 'and', 'of', 'the' etc. and a high weight to those words that occur only infrequently. In the extreme case if a word occurs in every document in the data base then its occurrence in one particular document is not going to tell us anything about the content of that document, while if a word occurs in only one document then it is likely to give some indication about the contents of that document. For more details of these, and other weighting functions, see Salton (1975). ◻

It is obviously important that any ranking system be not only theoretically sound but also capable of efficient implementation. The functions in the example in section 4.3.2 can all be calculated by a sequential pass through the entire file of vector representations. For large files this will be prohibitively expensive and a more efficient method is required. If the vectors are stored in a clustered file then we can restrict the search to the cluster that would contain the search request; the implementation of this is quite straightforward and is left as an exercise for the reader. If the system has a dictionary structure giving the list of occurrences of each individual word, then we can implement a ranking algorithm as follows.

4.3.3 Algorithm

Start ; term frequency weighting
Do While (more question terms)
      Get next question term
      Get list of documents containing term
      Do While (list contains documents not yet processed)
            Get next document vector
            Calculate sum of term frequencies
            Add to list of processed documents
            End-do
      End-do
      Sort list of documents by term frequency
End ◻

It is important to remember that this type of algorithm need not be based just on individual words. The basic elements of the vector representation can be words, word stems, phrases or thesaurus terms. This means that it is possible to adjust the type of representation so that the pattern matching can proceed as efficiently as possible. We have already indicated that the global weight of a term should be inversely related to its frequency. This can be taken a stage further by removing all high frequency words from the representation, though not from the original source text. Deleting common words such as 'and', 'of', 'the' etc. should cause few problems; but, as always it is possible to construct counter examples. Consider the two sentences

> Tom is in charge of Harry.
>
> Tom is in the charge of Harry.

More serious problems arise with words that carry little information on their own, but are very specific in combination. For example, 'top' and 'down' could easily be candidates for common word deletion but the phrase 'top down' is very specific and should be maintained in the analysed text. At the other extreme a word may be so infrequent that any search request involving the word will match only a handful of documents. In this case, the analysed text should contain the word stem or a broader thesaurus term rather than the original word. So, though the word frequency distribution in the original text may be far from uniform, the linguistic analysis can produce a representation based on a more uniformly distributed set of terms, by combining frequently occurring words into less frequent phrases and by replacing very infrequent words by more general thesaurus terms.

The standard pattern matching methods that we have discussed can be enhanced by the addition of a form of user feedback. The user's original search request was regarded as a document and the system presents the user with similar documents. The user is now in a position to say which of these documents he thinks matches his request and, on the basis of this information, the system can perform a search for documents which match those that the user has chosen. In the case of a general vector ranking system, if the original question, q, retrieved a list of documents, then the user can browse through the first few documents on the list and say which are relevant and which are not. The system can then construct a new search request

$$q' = q + a \sum r_i - b \sum s_j$$

where the r_i are the vector representations of the relevant documents, the s_j are the irrelevant documents and a and b are scaling factors such that

$$a + b = 1$$

This new search request should give a positive weight to all the relevant terms, a negative weight to any irrelevant terms and so provide a better matching function. Theoretical and experimental details of this method can be found in Yu *et al.* (1976).

There are other types of best-fit matching, apart from those covered by the definition of section 4.3.1 that can be applied to text processing systems. For example, the numeric representation based on the semantic co-ordinates of each word (section 2.4.5) requires a powerful algorithm for matching sequences of vectors. One possibility for this is to use Kolmogoroffs' general filter; it is outside the scope of this book to discuss this method and for more details the reader is referred to Teskey (1978). A second example of other types of matching is provided by the method of conceptor searching developed by Bing and Harvold (1977). Here the user specifies a number of concepts that the required document should contain, the system then ranks the documents according to the number of concepts that each document contains. At its simplest, with each concept corresponding to the occurrence of a given word, this is equivalent to the binary weighting (section 4.3.2.1) but in general the concepts may involve conditional retrieval of the type described below.

4.4 CONDITIONAL RETRIEVAL

In the best-fit type of algorithm the user specifies his request in natural language and the retrieval is based on a general comparison of the text of the request and the stored data. If the user can formalise his request by specifying a number of conditions that the data should satisfy, then this specification can be used as a basis for extracting the required information; this is known as conditional retrieval. Examples of the type of conditions that may be specified are: the author of the document should be Dr. Mount, the car registration should begin with CPK, the date of birth should be in 1950 etc. We shall start with the simplest condition, namely the presence of a given word in the text document; this gives rise to Boolean searching.

4.4.1 Definition
A Boolean search function is a logical combination (using **and, or** and **not**) of basic membership functions m_w where

$$m_w : D \rightarrow \{\text{true, false}\}$$

D is the set of documents in the data base and m_w takes the value **true** or **false** according as the word w does not occur in the document. □

Note that the basic membership function of a word is usually represented by the word itself. Once again, it is important to remember that the word may be a word stem, phrase or thesaurus term, as well as a simple word.

4.4.2 Example

Suppose we have four documents containing respectively:

(1) A user survey of information retrieval systems
(2) Some new information on the retrieval of nuclear by-products
(3) On-line interrogation of legal databases
(4) Information systems.

Then the Boolean search function

Information **and** Retrieval

will be **true** for documents one and two but **false** for the others. The retrieval of document two is an example of false co-ordination; the words 'information' and 'retrieval' do occur but not co-ordinated in the sense of 'information retrieval'. The user would probably regard this document as irrelevant and would not want to see it. On the other hand, he probably would want to see documents three and four; neither of these were retrieved, the search was too general to retrieve three and too specific to retrieve four. We shall see later how these problems can be overcome. □

The Boolean type of system forms the basis of many commercial text retrieval systems (Ashford 1980). It is simple to understand, it can be applied to a wide range of textual material and it can be implemented efficiently. The standard implementation uses a dictionary structure (as in section 3.4) to get a list of documents where each word occurs, these can then be logically combined to give the required answer. The standard algebraic notation (as in the example of section 4.4.2) can be converted to reverse Polish notation to simplify the subsequent evaluation. This is illustrated in the following algorithm. (It is assumed that the order of precedence of the logical operators is **not**, **and**, **or** and that **not** is a binary rather than a unary operator.)

4.4.3 Algorithm

> **Start** ; Boolean search function
> **Procedure** Eval ; Evaluates a Boolean combination of two reference lists
> > Get operator from operator stack
> > Get two operands from output stack
> > Evaluate Boolean operator
> > Move result to output stack
> > **End** Eval
>
> **Do while** (not end of search function)
> > Get next item
> > **Case of** (item)
> > Word   : Get pointer to reference list from dictionary
> > > Sort reference list, if necessary
> > > Move to output stack

Open bracket : move to operator stack
Close bracket : **Do while** (top of stack not open bracket) Eval
Terminator   : **Do while** (operator stack not empty) Eval
Operator   : **Do while** (operator on stack has higher precedence)
              Eval
              Move operator to stack

End-do

Stop □

One of the problems with the Boolean system as it stands is that the user has no explicit control over the amount of text that is presented to him. The system might retrieve 1000 documents and leave the user to browse through them all or it may not retrieve any documents at all; compare this with the case of the best-fit system where the user can require to see, say, the top ten documents closest to his request. The problem can be partially solved by the use of recall and precision devices; the former is intended to broaden the scope of the search and so retrieve more documents while the latter is intended to make the search more precise and so retrieve fewer documents. Thus a recall device should aim to replace infrequent and very specific words by more frequent, general words; the following is a list of some of the methods that may be used:

(i) Truncation: search for a word stem rather than a specific form of the word. This can be achieved by modifying the 'word' **case** in the algorithm in section 4.4.3 to get a combined reference list to all occurrences of the word stem.

(ii) Synonyms: search for a word and use its synonyms. This will require the user to specify the synonyms explicitly as

$$(s, \text{ or } s_2 \text{ or } \ldots \ldots \text{ or } s_n)$$

or the system to include such a list from an existing file of synonyms. Thus if 'information' and 'databases' were regarded as synonyms and also 'interrogation' and 'retrieval' then the search in section 4.4.2 would now retrieve document three as well.

(iii) Thesaurus: as with synonyms, a thesaurus can be used to find more general terms to include in a search request. It can also be used to find more specific words to replace existing general ones, and so it should also be regarded as a precision device.

A precision device aims not only to replace general words by more specific ones but also to restrict the scope of the search to specified areas of the text. Some of the methods available are discussed below.

(iv) Thesaurus: this has already been described in (iii) above.

(v) Fields: if the text analysis can divide the source text of each document into a number of predefined fields then it is possible to restrict the search to those fields. This is done by introducing a new operator **in** which takes a reference list as its first operand and a field name as its second and evaluates to give a list containing those references that occur in the specified field.

(vi) Collocation: if the reference lists are extended to give the exact location of each word within each document then the **and** operator can be made more precise by requiring that the words not only occur in the same document but also in a specified location relative to each other. The collocation operator is denoted by **and** $[m,n]$. This specifies that the two operands occur in the same document and that the second occurs between m and n words after the first $(m \leqslant n)$. The most important application of this is to search for a phrase, so if the search in section 4.4.2 were modified from

information **and** retrieval

to

information **and** $[1, 1]$ retrieval

then it would correctly reject document two.

For more information on these devices, see Teskey (1980).

From the preceding discussion it should be obvious that the more knowledge the user has of the structure of the analysed text, the more useful data he can extract from the system. Thus if the user wants to search a bibliographic data base for books by Mount, then a simple search might retrieve books about Mount St. Helens, but if the user knows that the text has been analysed into Author and Title fields, then he can issue the more precise search

Mount **in** Author

Similarly, when it comes to browsing through the retrieved documents he could just restrict himself to the Title field, and so find the titles of all books by Mount.

So far we have looked at some fairly simple conditions that can be used to specify which data should be extracted and presented to the user. These methods require only a limited linguistic analysis. If, however, a more detailed analysis has been performed then it is possible to specify more precise conditions for retrieval. If the data has been analysed and stored in a relational data base, then Codd (1971) has shown that the first order predicate calculus can be used to specify conditions for retrieving data from the data base. Recall that expressions in the first order predicate calculus consist of simple predicates combined with the Boolean operators **and, or** and **not** together with the existential and universal quantifiers $\forall$(for all) and $\exists$(there exists).

4.4.4 Definition

A relational search function (in the relational calculus) is an expression in the first order predicate calculus where the basic predicates are of the form

$$\text{relation-name. domain-name } comparison\text{-}operator \text{ value}$$

and *comparison-operator* is one of

$$=, \neq, <, \leqslant, >, \geqslant \quad \square$$

Thus a relational search function can be used to specify a subset of a given relation. In the language ALPHA (Codd 1971) the required relation is specified by a command of the form

Get relation-name : relational search function

This retrieves all those tuples in a given relation that specify the search function.

4.4.5 Example

Using the relational data base given in section 3.6 we can retrieve, shall we say, a list of the names of people employed as secretaries, by the following command

Get Employee: ∃ Job (Job.NI-number = Employee.NI-number

and Job.Description = 'secretary')

This statement says: get the set of Employee tuples such that for each Employee tuple there exists a Job tuple with NI-number equal to the employee's NI-number and whose job description is secretary.

This will retrieve each Employee tuple in full but since we want only the Name domain we can replace the '**Get** Employee' with a '**Get** Employee.Name'. □

The relational calculus is, theoretically, a very powerful tool for extracting data from a relational data base. However, it has proved difficult to implement and at the present time, there is little experience of such systems in a large production environment.

It seems likely that efficient implementations will be possible on content addressable memories (Anderson and Kain 1976). Similar, though less complete, facilities can be provided by the network and hierarchic approaches. Again, a discussion of these is outside the scope of this book and the interested reader is referred to Date (1975) and the reviews eidited by Sibley (1976).

4.5 RULE FOLLOWING

In the previous sections we have seen how the user can extract data from a text processing system by browsing through the data, by giving data similar to that which he wants or by specifying conditions that the required data must satisfy. We shall now look at another option, namely that the user gives the system a set of rules or instructions, the result of which is to present the required data to the user. This approach assumes that the system has a number of basic operations available to manipulate the data. This is best seen in the relational data base where the basic operators are projection and join.

4.5.1 Definition
If R is a relation on the domains $D_1, D_2, \ldots D_n$ then the projection of R on $D_i, D_j \ldots D_l$ is obtained by removing all but the specified domains from R and then removing any tuples that are now duplicated. The projection is denoted by

$$R[D_i, D_j \ldots D_l] \quad \square$$

4.5.2 Definition
If R is a relation on the domains $D_1, D_2, \ldots D_m$ and S is a relation on D_m, $D_{m+1}, \ldots D_n$, then the (natural) join of R and S is the relation on $D_1, D_2, \ldots D_n$ whose tuples are concatinations of R-tuples and S-tuples with a common D_m component. The join is denoted by

$$R * S \quad \square$$

These definitions form the basis of the relational algebra, which was developed by Codd (1971) and has been implemented in a number of systems. (See, for example, Todd 1976).

4.5.3 Example
To get the list, as in section 4.4.5, of names of people employed as secretaries, the instruction

$$((\text{Employee [name, NI-Number]}) * (\text{Job} * \text{`secretary'})) \text{ [name]}$$

will (i) Reorder the Employee relation so that it can be joined to the Job relation
   (ii) Join the Job relation with the single tuple 'secretary' to extract all tuples with this job description
   (iii) Join these two relations on the NI-number domain to get the name of each secretary.
   (iv) Project this last relation onto the Name domain to give the required list. $\square$

It is clear that writing rules such as these needs not only skill but also a detailed knowledge of the structure of the data base. It is possible, however, to package these detailed rules so that they can be used by people without this skill and knowledge. This can be achieved by providing multiple views of the data, each one tailored to a particular user application. Every view corresponds to a new relation, but these relations are defined only by name and are not evaluated until required. This avoids any problems of storage space and updates that would arise from having multiple copies of the same data.

4.5.4 Example

Using the prefix N! to indicate that a relation is used by name rather than value, we can define the relation

Joblist = ((N! Employee [name, NI-number] *N! Job)) [name, description]

Then the command

Joblist * 'secretary'

will evaluate the Joblist relation and then join it to the single tuple 'secretary' to give the required list of names.

A similar effect can be obtained by the use of a macro processor. Recall that a macro processor is a piece of software for replacing one sequence of characters, the macro call, in a source text by another pre-defined (and usually much longer) sequence of characters, the macro body. The macro body may contain dummy parameters which are replaced by the actual values in the macro call. (For more details see Brown 1974). Thus the command in section 4.5.3 could be replaced by a macro call of the form

Joblist (secretary)

where **Joblist** is a macro name whose macro body corresponds to the original command, but with a dummy parameter in place of the actual value 'secretary'. It is now possible to call the macro with any job description as the actual parameter and obtain a list of names of people in that particular job.

The Boolean search functions described in section 4.4 can also be used as a basis for rule following systems. The main difference is that whereas the results of relational operators can themselves be used as input for further operations this is not so for Boolean operators. A typical sequence of rules would contain just a search function and a display command. Once again, this can be packaged as a macro to simplify the user interface.

4.5.6 Example

Define a macro called **Autlist** which contains the two commands

Search £1 **in** Author

Display Title

where £1 denotes a dummy parameter. Then the macro call

Autlist (Mount)

will display all the titles of books written by Mount. Compare this with the example in section 4.5.4. □

In many cases, this pattern of search and display is all that is required. It may be desirable, however, to present the data in a different format; in this

case, a report generator or formatter can be used to process the retrieved data
before it is presented to the user.

4.6 DEDUCTIVE METHODS

Some of the rule following methods discussed in the previous section already
have a limited deductive capability built into them. For example, the **Joblist**
macro can find the NI-number of all the secretaries and use that information to
deduce the names of all the secretaries. This deduction is built into the macro
itself but a general system should be able to generate these deductive rules
from the data itself. Consider, for example, the two sentences

> All men are mortal.

> Socrates is a man.

and the question

> Is Socrates mortal?

It should be possible to recognise the first sentence as a general rule and use that
rule to infer the correct answer to the question. The first problem is in representing the universal quantifier 'all'. As yet there is no wholly satisfactory way
of analysing and storing text involving the logical quantifiers, though the preference semantics developed by Wilks (1975) provides one possible method. Even if
we ignore the problems caused by the logical quantifiers we are still left with
the problem of trying to organise the large number of apparently trivial rules
that go to make up our view of the world and our use of language. Consider
the sentences

> Paris is the capital of France.

> France is in Europe.

and the question

> Is Paris in Europe?

In order to deduce the answer to this question the system must use rules of the
form

> **If** A is the capital of B **then** A is in B.

> **If** A is in B **and** B is in C **then** A is in C.

Thus any deductive system must have a library of such rules. This means that the
universe of discourse must be limited to such an extent that it is possible to
enumerate all the rules that make up its world view. It is then possible to apply
the techniques of automated theorem proving, based on a heuristic search to try
to find a chain of inference that leads to the required data. Details of the theory

can be found in Robinson (1965), and an experimental application in Winograd (1972).

It should be noted that there are serious problems in implementing this type of system. Because of this, more interest has been focussed on frame based systems. Here, the deductive capability is inherent in the structure of the frames and their attached procedures. Thus, in section 3.6.2, the rule that a traveller is a client is implied by the procedure to link the client to the traveller. In this way, it may be possible to build up a large knowledge structure without having the overhead of exhaustive searching and backtracking. A possible application of this is described by Shank *et al.* (1981).

4.7 SUMMARY

In this chapter we have looked at methods of extracting data from the various storage structures that were described in the previous chapter. The general term 'data extraction' has been used to cover a whole spectrum of methods including those usually applied to document retrieval and fact retrieval. Some of the methods have been tried and tested in practical systems while others are still in the experimental stage, in particular the relational calculus and the deductive systems. Once again, it is the simpler forms of data extraction which have the wider application. Before we look at how the methods discussed in this and the previous chapters can be combined into a complete text processing system it is necessary to study one further item, namely the user interface.

5

User Interfaces

Houses are built to live in and not to look on;
therefore let use be preferred before uniformity,
except where both may be had.

Francis Bacon
Of Building

5.1 USER REQUIREMENTS

In the previous chapters we have discussed various aspects of text processing
and described various algorithms that are used in this field. It is, however,
important to realise that the ultimate aim of a text processing system is to
provide a tool for the user, and so the ways in which the user can interact
with the system will be just as important as the algorithms used to implement
the system. It is worth considering some general requirements that apply to all
user interfaces, not just text processing systems:

(i) Ease of use — the interface should match, as closely as possible, the
user's preferred method of working.

(ii) Helpful informative and diagnostic messages — the system should keep
the user informed of what it is doing, and relate error messages to the
user's view of the system.

(iii) Flexibility — it should be possible to tailor the interface to meet a
number of different user requirements.

(iv) Economy — the number of commands that the user is required to
learn, and the number of keystrokes required for any given command
should be kept to a minimum.

In a text processing system there are four main areas where the user interface
is important. They are:

(i) Text input
(ii) Text modification
(iii) Search formulation
(iv) Data output.

The first two functions involve writing information into the data base while the second two involve only reading from the data base. These functions may, in general, be performed by different users and we can classify users by the type of access they have to the data base: read only or read/write access. There is a third class of user, the data base administrator, who is responsible for the overall administration of the text processing system. His role will be discussed in the next chapter; in the following sections we shall see how the general principles of user interfaces can be applied to the four areas of text processing listed above.

5.2 TEXT INPUT

It is clear that the usefulness of any text processing system will depend on the text that has been entered into the system. Thus, in the design of any text processing system considerable attention should be paid to the methods used for text input. These methods fall into two classes depending on whether or not the text already exists in machine readable form. In the former case, the text will have to be converted into the format required by the new system while in the latter case the user will have to input the text by means of a keyboard.

We will consider, firstly, the direct input of text from a keyboard. There are three main types of method that can be used:

    (i) Free format
    (ii) Line by line prompting
    (iii) Form filling.

Free format text input, as its name implies, gives the user complete freedom entering text into the system. This has the obvious advantage that the user is not constrained as to the length or type of text he can input. It does mean, however, that the user must supply any control characters or markers that the system may require. This may be no more than a single system marker to indicate where one document stops and the next begins, or it may be a complicated set of tags, fields and sub-field delimiters such as required by the MARC format for bibliographic data (Irvine 1972). (Some sample source text, complete with system markers is given in Appendix II). Since nearly all computer operating systems provide some facilities to input and edit text files, these could be used to support free text input to text processing systems. In some cases, however, these facilities are intended to be used only by experienced computer personnel and would not be suitable for use in text processing systems. So there may be a need to provide a separate text editing facility as part of the whole text processing system. While this adds to the overall size of the system it has the advantage that the editing function can be more closely integrated with the rest of the system. In either case, one must include software to check that the user has correctly entered the required system markers. (We shall discuss checking the actual text later in this section.) Because of these difficulties, free format text input is used mainly for the automatic input of text already in machine readable form.

If it is required to enter a number of text documents with a similar structure, then this can be achieved by using some type of prompting system. Line by line prompting issues the user with a sequence of prompts for each of the fields required in the original structure. This overcomes the problems of entering system markers, while retaining much of the flexibility of free format input. In the simplest case where the text is just divided up into a number of documents, the system could issue a prompt of the form:

Enter text of document, terminated by a blank line

The user would then be free to enter any text and on terminating the text as indicated the required system marker would automatically be added.

For more complicated structures it is possible to provide a proforma which specifies the required format of the text, and use it as a basis for prompting the user. The proforma must contain, as a minimum, two types of entry:

(i) Space for user data with initial prompt and required terminator. In the following examples the syntax

$<$ prompt; terminator $>$

is used for the input of user data; some of the valid terminators are

CR – carriage return, that is, single line input
null – null line (for multi-line text)

(ii) Text to be retained 'as is', including system markers. In the following examples such text is enclosed in double quotes thus

"text"

The following algorithm can be used in conjuction with such proforma.

5.2.1 Algorithm

    Start ; Line by line prompting
    Do While (more lines in proforma)
        Get next line from proforma
        Case (type of line)
            User data : Issue prompt
                    Get next line from user
                    Do While (not terminator)
                        Copy to output file
                        Get next line from user
                  End do
            Text : Copy to output file
  End do
  Stop □

This basic algorithm can be extended in a number of ways; we shall consider two possibilities. Firstly, the proforma could include calls to other, named, proforma to input standard sequences of text, which could be indicated by a line of the form:

> **Get** proforma-name

Secondly, any line in the proforma could have an associated condition which had to be satisfied before that line would be included. At its simplest this could be a **case** statement dependent on the value of the last user input.

5.2.2 Example

Consider a library loans system which has to input details of books and borrowers for various types of transactions such as the loan and return of a book. This can be achieved by the following three proformas:

```
TRANS        :   < Enter transaction code ; CR >
                 Case
                    (Loan, L)    :   get BORROWER
                                     get BOOK
                    (Return, R) :   get BOOK
                 "** END"

BOOK         :   "** ACC"
                 < Accession number ; CR >
                 < Copy ; CR >

BORROWER :       "** NAM"
                 < Name ; CR >
                 < Address, terminated by blank line ; null >
```

A possible input sequence might be: (computer prompts shown in italic, carriage return shown as < CR >).

> *Enter transaction code L* < CR >
> *Name* F. N. Teskey < CR >
> *Address, terminated by blank line*
> Department of Computer Science < CR >
> University of Manchester < CR >
> < CR >
> *Accession number* 12469 < CR >
> *Copy* 1 < CR >

The corresponding output file would be

> *L*
> ** NAM
> F. N. Teskey
> Department of Computer Science
> University of Manchester
> ** ACC
> 12469
> 1
> ** END □

With the advent of visual display units with full screen support, it is possible to combine a number of these individual prompts into a single form which can be filled in by the user and transmitted to the computer in a single interaction. Thus the BORROWER proforma in section 5.2.2 could be replaced by a form as in Fig. 5.1. This is displayed to the user and he is then free to enter the required text in the shaded areas. This is usually faster than line by line prompting since all the text can be entered in a single interaction; the disadvantage, however, is that it limits the amount of text that can easily be entered into any given field.

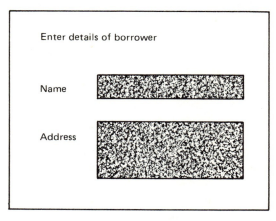

Fig. 5.1 – Borrower form.

We have considered the direct input of text from a keyboard, but in many applications the text that is to be input to the system already exists in machine readable form. There are four possible sources of such machine readable text:

   (i) optical character recognition (OCR)
  (ii) computer typesetting
 (iii) word processing
 (iv) other text data bases.

OCR techniques are still somewhat limited and require a good clear type-face (Anderson 1977). Improvements are still being made and in the future it should be possible to use OCR to capture text that would not otherwise be available in machine readable form. It is important to realise, however, that with the growing use of computer typesetting and word processing a lot of text will originate in machine readable form. Also, with the increasing number of text data bases, it is often possible to capture some of the data required for a new system from existing data bases. (Voice input is possible but at present it appears to be limited to a vocabulary of a few hundred words spoken by one or two known voices, Lea 1980).

In all these cases, although the text is in machine readable form there may still be problems in getting it into the new system. Firstly the text may have to be converted to a character code and format that is acceptable to the host computer, and secondly old system markers may need to be removed and re-placed by new ones. Both these operations can be quite complex and require considerable software development. In general each case will have to be dealt with on its own merits. To give some idea of what could be involved in a simple case, two distinct input formats are illustrated in Appendix II.

5.3 TEXT MODIFICATION

Once the text has been entered into the system it may still require a certain amount of modification. This can consist of automatically generating additional text, such as the current date, expanding abbreviated codes into their full form, making standard changes to the text, as well as correcting errors in the text. This modification may continue throughout the whole lifetime of the data and so it will be necessary not only to modify text coming into the system but also to extract text from the system, modify it and replace it in the data base.

In many applications there will be a need to add extra data to the original source text. For example, a bibliographic data base may require the addition of unique accession numbers to each document. This could be performed manually, but it would prove very difficult to coordinate a number of users at different locations trying to allocate unique accession numbers from a single sequence. In cases such as these it makes sense to let the text processing system generate the additional text. In the main this will consist of information such as unique identification numbers, current date, time of day, identification of the source of the text etc.

As well as adding information to the text, it may be necessary to make some standard changes to the text. These changes could involve altering varia-tions of a word to a standard form, expanding abbreviations to their full form, reordering parts of the text to produce a standard format etc. Consider, for example, a business data base containing details of a company's orders and invoices. The names and addresses of some individual firms will be repeated many times and the user may have input a short code rather than the full name and address of these firms. Thus given a table of codes and their expanded form the system can perform a simple table look-up and replace the code with the required full text.

Before the input text is analysed it should be checked as thoroughly as possible. But even after it has been analysed and stored, the text may still contain mistakes or require updating. Thus it should be possible to modify text, not only as it is entered into the system, but also once it has been stored in the data base. But, even though the system may have this facility, the source text should still be validated as fully as possible. There is a certain amount of checking that can be performed automatically by the text processing system, and obviously the more precisely the allowable inputs are defined then the more input validation is possible. In a free text system, one of the main problems is to check the spelling, not only to correct mis-spellings but also to identify acceptable spelling variations. This latter function is particularly important in systems where the source text has both American and English origins, since there is then a wide range of different spellings, for example 'colour' and 'color'. Unfortunately, there are no hard and fast rules that can be applied to identify mis-spellings; the most useful technique appears to be that of vocabulary logging. Once a corpus of text has been input and manually checked, then the system can construct a dictionary containing the full vocabulary of that text. Each word in any new text to be added to the corpus can then be checked against the existing vocabulary and any new words brought to the attention of the user; the user can then decide whether these are valid new words to be added to the vocabulary or mis-spellings to be corrected. While this works fairly well, it is not ideal and, in particular, it will not identify mis-spellings of a word which results in another quite acceptable word, for example, 'He took the 9.05 town drain to Oxford.' (Where 'town drain' should be 'down train'.) A more drastic solution is to fix the allowable vocabulary in advance. It is then possible to verify every word against this fixed vocabulary. This solution is very attractive in those systems where detailed semantic information is required for all valid words, since the semantic information can be added in to the dictionary when the original vocabulary is created.

If the text contains numeric values, then these should, if possible, be checked. If the values correspond to some known attribute, then it should be possible to obtain likely maximum and minimum values and notify the user of any values outside this range. So, for example, an attempt to enter the height of a person as '50 feet' should be pointed out to the user as a probable mistake. Note that it may not be possible to identify this until after the text has been analysed.

Once all, or at least most, of the mistakes have been identified the source text must be edited to the correct form. There are three main types of editor that can be used.

(i) positional — the editor maintains a pointer to the current position in the text, this pointer can be moved forward (and in some cases backward) to indicate where text is to be added or deleted.

(ii) contextual — the editor recognises text to be altered on the basis of its (unique) context, for example

replace | This is here | This was here |

replaces the word 'is' with the word 'was' in the phrase 'This is here'.

(iii) full screen — the editor presents the text to the user on a visual display unit (VDU), the user can then over-type the incorrect text to produce a correct version.

Needless to say, any editor can contain any combination of these features, and the most powerful editors are those employing all three methods.

It must be remembered that text already in the data base may need to be modified. So, whether we are using an operating system editor or one incorporated in the text processing system, it is essential to provide a simple interface to extract the text from the data base, present it to the user for editing and replace the edited text in the data base.

Finally, the input and modification of the text require that the user has permission to write to the data base. This is especially important if there are many users with access to a single data base. We will discuss this problem later in the general context of data administration.

5.4 SEARCH FORMULATION

In Chapter 4 we described a number of methods for extracting data from a text processing system. We did not, however, discuss in detail how the user should formulate his search and present it to the system. There are three main methods that are available:

(i) menu selection
(ii) command driven
(iii) natural language based.

For each of the retrieval strategies that we have discussed, it is possible to use any of the above methods of search formulation but as we proceed we shall see that for certain applications some are more suitable than others.

The idea behind an interface based on a menu selection system is that, at every stage of the search session, the user chooses the next action from a 'menu', a list of available options. The menu can be presented either line by line, or as a full screen display. This method of searching is obviously suited to the inexperienced user, since the system can provide him with the maximum possible help. So, as one would expect, it has been applied to browsing methods and in particular hierarchical browsing. Here the options open to the user at any stage are simply of the choice of one of a number of sub-trees available for searching. Thus each menu consists of descriptions of the sub-trees that can be reached from the current node, and the user chooses which one he wants to search. A menu selection system has also been applied to Boolean searching; see, for example, the User Cordial Interface (UCI) developed by Goldstein and Ford (1978). For the inexperienced user the freedom of searching that is available with the Boolean system can be an embarrassment and a menu system can be used to limit and direct this choice. For example, in a bibliographic system it may be possible to search an author, title, abstract, date and place of publication etc, but for many users all that is required is author or title; thus a menu system can offer the user these alternatives and formulate the search accordingly. A menu based system can also be used in conjunction with a thesaurus to select preferred terms for searching (either best-fit or Boolean). The principle is just the same as for hierarchical browsing: the user is presented with a list of head terms, selects the one he is interested in and follows a chain of 'narrower term' pointers till he finds a **preferred term** that describes his request (or part of it).

We have shown how a menu-driven system can be used to formulate a single search; in practice, however, the user will need to perform a number of successive searches to fulfil his original requirement. Since the aim of a menu system is to guide the user, it must provide a means of submitting a sequence of searches, and examining the output from those searches. This will require a second set of menus concerned with data output and a primary menu to choose between the search and display functions. An example of the operation of this in the UCI system is given in Appendix III.

The principle of a command driven interface is to allow the user as much freedom and control of the system as is possible. This means that the user must have some understanding of the system, and in particular, of the functions and commands he will require. As we have seen, conditional and rule following methods expect the user to have some understanding of the data base, and so it is in these areas that command languages are most appropriate. The command language can have one of a number of different syntax structures; we shall consider just one, (the prefix notation) which is commonly used. (An illustration of this syntax is given in the sample STATUS session in Appendix III). The standard form of command is

<command name> <required parameters> <optional parameters>

In this format, each command can have a number of parameters, some of which the user must supply and the others are optional and default values can be supplied by the system. The individual parameters can be identified either by position in a parameter list or by a keyword followed by the actual parameter. Since, in general, a keyword could be mistaken for an optional positional parameter it is not recommended that these two methods of parameter recognition be combined in a single command. Finally, if the user omits any of the required parameters the system should be able to prompt for these missing parameters. Thus all the information required to input and analyse such a command language can be stored in a command dictionary, with an entry for each command as shown in Fig. 5.2.

Command name
Number of required parameters
Prompt for first required parameter
Prompt for second required parameter

. . . .

Number of optional parameters
Keyword/positional flag
Default value (and keyword) for first optional parameter
Default value (and keyword) for second optional parameter

. . . .

Fig. 5.2 – Command dictionary.

The following algorithm, using this dictionary structure, can be used to input and analyse the above type of command language.

5.4.1 Algorithm

Start ; command interpreter
Read in command line
Get command name
Get structure of command from dictionary
Do I = 1 **to** (number of required parameters)
      If (Parameter I present) **then** get parameter I
                        else   issue prompt I
                              get parameter I
      End if
End do
Case
      (keyword) : **Do while** (more parameters)
                      Get keyword
                      Get corresponding parameter
              End do
              Get remaining default values
      (positional) : **Do** I = 1 **to** (number of optional parameters)
                  If (parameter I present)   **then** get value
                                        else get default
              End if
              End do
Stop

We mentioned in section 4.5 the use of macro processors in search formulation and the above algorithm can be used as the basis of analysing such macro calls. A macro call generally has the form

$$\% \text{ macro-name (parameter-1, parameter-2, } \ldots \text{ parameter-}n)$$

where % is a warning character to indicate the start of a macro and the brackets are used to delimit the parameter list. If the following conditions are met:

(i) the macro name is the first item on the line
(ii) the last parameter is the last item on the line, and
(iii) the macro name is different from all possible command names

then the user can omit the warning character % and the delimiting brackets since these are implicit in the start and end of line. Thus, the macro appears to the user like any other command, the system realises it is a macro since it is not a valid command, and the above algorithm can be used to analyse the macro call. This use of macros allows great flexibility in that, given a set of basic commands it is possible to build up a set of macro commands that are tailored to a particular user's requirements (Teskey 1980). The one drawback is that, although the command input has been tailored to the user, the output of messages and errors remains the same and may not be related to the original macro command. This problem can be partly overcome by adding to each macro body a list of system messages that may be produced and the appropriate action to take for each message. (Possible actions would include issuing a new macro command, issuing a macro specific message or just suppressing the original message.)

Finally, we come to the use of natural language for search formulation. If the user expresses his information request in natural language then this can be used as a basis for extracting the required data from the system. It should be clear to the reader that this is an ideal method for search formulation for best-fit systems; it is, indeed, commonly used. See, for example, the Current Information Transfer in English (CITE) system developed by Doszkocs and Rapp (1979); an illustration of this system is given in Appendix III.

Natural language input has also been applied to rule following and deductive systems (Woods *et al.* 1972). This requires a detailed linguistic analysis of the user's search request to determine what data is required, and as we indicated in Chapter 2, this is only possible in a small well-defined universe of discourse. Thus, though such systems may seem to present the user with a very simple interface there is a danger that the user will expect the system to understand much more than it has in fact been designed to do. So it is important to realise that despite the apparent attractions of natural language in search formulation it has, at the moment, certain practical limitations.

5.5 DATA OUTPUT

The output of data to the user will depend both on the form of the source text and the method of data extraction that has been employed. For browsing, best-fit and conditional retrieval, the data output will be part of the source text, possibly edited and reformatted; for deductive systems the output will be some external representation of part of the analysed text. In the latter case, if the data required is simple numeric or character data then there is no problem in presenting it to the user, but if the data required is textual then the natural language text will have to be constructed from an internal representation. Note that this is related to the problem of language generation in machine translation; one possible method of tackling the problem is presented by Wilks (1975). For the rest of this section we will concentrate on the display of the original text.

If the user wishes to display a number of documents then he has various options available to him. He can:

   (i) output the full text or selected parts of the text
  (ii) output the text as it is or in an edited version
 (iii) specify the order in which the documents are to be displayed
  (iv) specify calculations to be performed on indicated numeric fields
   (v) specify the destination of the output text.

If the user does not want to see the full text then he can either specify to the system which parts of the text he is interested in or he can leave it to the system to decide. The most that the system can do is to try and identify those parts of the text that are similar to the user's request. A simple, and perhaps the most useful, algorithm is to output the text in the neighbourhood of each occurrence of each word in the user's search request.

It is possible to perform a wide range of editing on the output text. If there are any standard abbreviations in the text then these can be expanded, the text can be reformatted and, if necessary, displayed in a proforma. In addition we can combine text from several documents into a single display. For example, in a personnel data base, rather than get out a separate display for each employee the user may want a combined display as shown in Fig. 5.3.

Name	Smith J	Jones R
Job	Secretary	Electrician . . .
Pay	–	£150

Fig. 5.3 – Combined data output.

In browsing and best-fit systems the order in which documents are presented is well defined. In conditional retrieval the order is undefined and so the user is free to specify any desired ordering. Typically the order will be either chronological, alphabetical or numerical based on some pre-defined key or keys in the text.

If the text contains readily identifiable numeric data then, given a set of documents, it may be possible to identify corresponding numeric values and perform simple calculations on them. In the personnel file a typical example would be to calculate the total wages payed to a group of workers.

Finally, the user should be able to indicate where the data is to be output. Many text processing systems are based on a central computer linked to clusters of remote terminals. In such an environment the user would have three possible output destinations:

(i) local visual display unit for small quantities of transient data
(ii) local (slow) printers for small quantities of data required semi-permanently
(iii) central (fast) printer for bulk output of data.

In addition it may be desirable to send data to temporary or permanent operating system files for further processing.

These facilities can be combined into a comprehensive report generation facility. This requires:

(i) a proforma containing some standard text and a number of slots to contain data extracted from the data base, and
(ii) a set of data extraction commands, one for each slot in the proforma.

Sections of the proforma may have to be repeated using data from a number of related documents. Thus the proforma may be divided into a number of sections with a search command at the start of each section to identify the set of documents required. The following algorithm can be used to generate reports based on this type of proforma.

5.5.1 Algorithm

```
Start ; Report Generator
Do while (more sections in proforma)
        Get next section
        Get corresponding search command
        Retrieve relevant documents
        For (each relevant document) Do
                Do while (more slots in section)
                        Get next slot
                        Execute corresponding data extraction command
                        Store data in current slot
                End do
                Output section
        End for
End do
Stop. □
```

5.5.2 Example

Consider the case of a library loans system which contains details of books that have been lent out to various readers. The proforma in Fig. 5.4 could be used to produce a set of overdue notices for books that should be returned.

Section $<$ overdue $>$
            "To" $<$ name $>$
                      $<$ address $>$
            "The following book is overdue and should be returned"
            "to the Library"
            "Author" $<$ author $>$
            "Title" $<$ title $>$

Fig. 5.4 – Proforma for overdue notices.

This proforma contains just one section, the search command at the beginning of the section is indicated by angled brackets, in this case it is a macro command 'overdue' which would retrieve all the documents relating to books which were due back today. The slots in the proforma are indicated by angled brackets containing the data extraction commands; in this case there are four macro commands ('name', 'address', 'author' and 'title') which extract the required parts of each document. A typical output from this is shown in Fig. 5.5. □

To   F. N. Teskey
            Department of Computer Science
The following book is overdue and should be returned
to the Library
Author   Beveridge J. I.
Title   Guidelines for the application of hearing tests

Fig. 5.5 – Output for overdue notices.

5.6 USER AIDS

In any text processing system there will be a number, possibly quite a large number, of users who will require some assistance in using the system. The help required will be concerned mainly with the operation of the system and the content of the data base. The provision of comprehensive, and comprehensible, documentation and detailed user training is essential, but in addition there is a need for help to be available to the user while he is actually using the system — on-line aid. The standard method of giving information about using the system is by means of a HELP function. This should provide a general introduction to the system, a list of functions that are available and detailed information on those functions. Providing information on the content of the data base is more difficult. But, since the system is being used to store text there is no reason why each data base should not contain a number of documents with a description of the data base itself. These documents should be stored at some well defined point in the system to enable the user to access them readily. Beyond this, the type of information that can usefully be provided will depend on the methods used for analysing and storing the text. Thus a cluster based system should provide a summary of the various clusters that have been formed, a thesaurus based system should provide a facility for browsing through the thesaurus, a free text system should provide a means of looking at the current vocabulary etc. The exact facilities required will depend on the collective user requirements.

In systems with a large number of users it is often helpful if each user can build his own view of the system. We have already discussed this for relational data bases in section 4.5.4 and for command languages in section 5.4. It is still possible to do this type of tailoring in other areas but more work is involved. For example, in a thesaurus based system, if one group of users wanted a slightly different set of thesaurus terms, then these extra terms would have to be added in to the relevant documents and made invisible to all other users.

Finally, if a user is frequently searching a data base he may want to keep information from one search to the next. A typical example of this is in current awareness — a user has a particular interest and, on a regular basis, wants to extract all new information in his given field of interest. This can be achieved by providing a facility to store any search request for future use.

5.7 SUMMARY

In this chapter we have returned to the original notion of a text processing system as a tool for the user. We have looked at what requirements this places on the user interface with respect to text input, modification, searching and data output. In each case a distinction has to be made between a simple fixed interface for a naive user and a complex powerful interface for more experienced users. The use of a proforma for input prompting, command macros for searching and a report generator for output seem to provide one possible compromise. In all cases the main requirements are for ease of use and helpful diagnostic messages. In addition to this there is also a need for some overall control of the text processing system and we shall discuss this in the next chapter on data base management.

6

Data Base Management

*Integrity without knowledge is weak and
useless, and knowledge without integrity
is dangerous and dreadful.*

Samuel Johnson
Rasselas

6.1 THE NEED FOR MANAGEMENT

We have already emphasised the fact that a text processing system should be
regarded as a tool which is used to help perform a given task. The user needs to
know how to work the tool but not how it works. Whilst it may be possible
to reach this ideal in a small single-user system, the problem becomes much
more acute in a large multi-user environment. In the latter case each user will
expect the system to:

(i) perform his particular task without interference from other users
(ii) maintain a correct, comprehensive and up to date data base
(iii) provide assistance to overcome any problems that may arise.

As well as this, the user does not want to be, and indeed need not be, concerned
with the problems of implementing and running the text processing system on
his particular computer hardware. In short, an operational text processing
system is complex and expensive and needs some form of management to
ensure that the user is provided with all the facilities he requires.

The management of a text processing system covers a wide range of activi-
ties. For a start, installing such a system will require new or enhanced computer
facilities, with all the management problems that it involves. After that the
software itself will have to be installed, tested and maintained. A discussion of
the problems involved in this area can be found in Wessel (1980); for the rest of
this chapter we will assume that all this has been achieved and concentrate on
the management of the data base itself. We will consider, firstly, the management decisions involved in designing and building a data base, and then go on to
look at the role of the data base manager in maintaining the text in the system

and protecting the user's data from unauthorised access. Finally, we will look at the additional support that the user may require from the data base management.

6.2 DATA BASE DESIGN

The efficiency and success of any text processing system will depend very much on the decisions taken during the initial design of the data base. During the development of the system it may be possible to change some of the decisions that were made at the design stage, but once the system is in widespread use there will be considerable inertia to any changes that are not upward compatible, that is, changes that cause the user to alter his method of using the system. This means that enhancements to the system are often made on an ad hoc basis which, whilst producing a temporary solution, cause more problems in the long run. Thus any time spent improving the design of the system is time well spent, and it is important to try and ensure that the design will meet all the user's present, and foreseeable, information requirements.

There are two central parts in the design of any text processing system, the text to be stored in the system and the software that is to be used to process it. The former depends on the field of interest to the user's general information requirement, and the latter on the type of enquiries and results the user expects from the system. It may be necessary to design and build either or both of these from scratch, but if an existing design matches the user's requirements then it makes sense to use it. Note that the existing system may require some modification before it is suitable for the intended application. Also, since many different applications will require a similar type of system, some suitable software might well already exist. A method of deciding how to proceed with the design of a text processing system is given in section 6.2.1. (The problems of data integrity, data security and user support will also affect the design of the system — these will be discussed later in this chapter).

6.2.1 Algorithm

[See diagram overleaf]

It is unlikely that any existing system will exactly match the user's requirements, but with some modification of an existing system and of the user's requirements it may be possible to come to a suitable compromise. If major changes would be required, or if the user or the system would be forced into an unfamiliar method of working, then some alternative should be sought. For example, Fig. 6.1 shows that it is possible to instruct a Boolean system to produce a type of ranked output, but this can not be recommended for a working system.

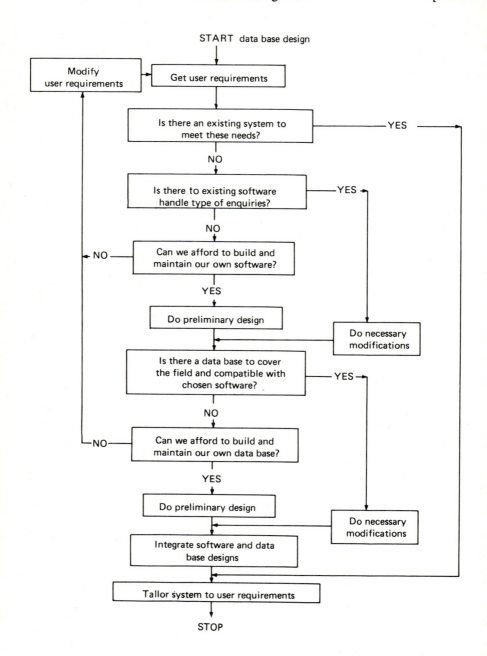

search a **and** b **and** c
display
search ((a **and** b) **or** (b **and** c) **or** (c **and** a))
        not (a **and** b **and** c)
display
search (a **or** b **or** c) **not**
        ((a **and** b) **or** (b **and** c) **or** (c **and** a))
display

Fig. 6.1 – Ranked output from a Boolean system.

In some cases the modifications may be no more than simple changes to the text processing system, for example, changing the set of concordable characters used in the lexical analysis or the similarity coefficient used in the ranking algorithm or the proformas used for report generation.

Once the general content of the data has been fixed the next major concern is with the structure of the data. The text in the system consists of units of data (words, numeric values and character strings) and these are grouped together into units of information (records, fields, documents etc). In designing the data base the following decisions will have to be made:

(i) what is the definition of a basic unit of data
(ii) how are these units related to each other
(iii) how do they combine to form units of information
(iv) how are these units of information related to each other.

6.2.2 Example

As an example of the design of a data base consider the problem of building a pharmaceutical system for a large teaching hospital. The hospital may have several requirements for such a system:

(i) to minimise the cost of drugs prescribed and the number of different brands of similar drugs that are used
(ii) to provide rapid identification of tablets, drugs etc to treat poison and attempted suicide cases
(iii) to develop an experimental scheme for automatic prescription of drugs
(iv) to produce regular and ad hoc reports on the use of drugs in the hospital.

It is unlikely that there is an existing system which would meet all these needs and so we must consider designing a new system. There may be systems which would perform each of the individual functions and so the hospital's requirements could be met by four different systems. The advantage of this approach it that it uses existing software, the disadvantage is that it involves considerable duplication in text input, data maintenance and user training. A decision such as this would obviously require careful consideration; in this example we will assume that the data base manager has decided in favour of a single integrated system. Such a system should make use of existing algorithms and software wherever possible. In particular, the expected type of enquiries could probably be met by a conditional retrieval facility for item (i), a best match facility for items (ii) and (iii) and a report generator for item (iv). Software for these functions should be available, and after it has been tailored to this particular application the next step is to look at the data base. The information required for items (ii) and (iii) will probably already be available from manufacturers' information sheets and the medical literature, whilst the data for items (i) and (iv) should be available from the hospital's own records. It then remains to integrate this data base with the proposed software and tailor the whole system to the user's requirements. This will involve such items as adjusting the lexical analysis to deal with chemical names and formulae, adding pharmaceutical and medical terms into the thesaurus and generating the proformas for the required reports. As we have already indicated the basic unit of data would be either a word or a chemical formulae; it would probably prove useful to have a thesaurus to provide links between related data items. The basic unit of information would be a document containing all the information about a given drug: different brand names and cost, physical description, use, side effects, details of overdoses etc. □

Obviously the detailed design of the data base will depend on the actual software used. However, the general aim of the data base manager remains the same — namely to try and design a system that matches the user requirements as closely as possible.

6.3 DATA BASE BUILDING

Like data base design, many of the points about data base buildings are implicit in the previous discussions of text processing systems. In this section we will try and bring these ideas together and look at them from the point of view of the data base manager. Building a data base involves not only gathering together all the source text required for the system but also collecting any data required for the linguistic analysis and for any user aids in the system. We will look at each of these in turn.

The original source text forms the core of any text processing system and we have already discussed its impact on the overall design of the system. As well as defining the scope and structure of the text to be stored the data base manager is responsible for seeing that the text is correctly stored in the system. The general scope of the system will have been set out in the design stage, but in any system there may be day to day decisions on whether or not a particular text should be included. Similarly, though a general editorial policy has been decided at the design stage it will almost certainly have to be kept under review as the data base is built. If the text is being typed directly into the system one can leave the simple editorial control to the typist. But in this and other cases the data base manager should check the validity of the text either on a random or exhaustive basis. Once a new batch of text has been input and is ready to be stored in the system, the manager must decide when the data base should be updated. The system may allow only one update job to proceed at any one time and may even prevent ordinary users from searching the data base whilst the update is in progress. One possible approach is to batch up all the updates and run them as a single job overnight, or when the system is not required for searching. We will see later that this has benefits for data integrity but obviously it is not acceptable when the system must provide up-to-date information. The data base manager will have to decide on the update schedule that best meets his user's requirements. Note that as the data base grows, the input and update may need to be changed to cope with new data structures or changing user requirements.

The analysis of the text will require some standard linguistic information, sometimes called the knowledge base of the system. Some of this information, such as the set of concordable characters, will have been built in to the original design, whilst other information, such as common words and thesaurus entries, will be built up in parallel with the main data base. The system should provide the manager with a number of tools to monitor the growth of the data base, and using the results of this monitoring, to look at and, if necessary, change the knowledge base. The simplest example of this is to look at the new words that have been added to the vocabulary, the data base manager can then decide what information the system needs to know about these words e.g. are there any synonyms for the word already in the system, does the word need an entry in the thesaurus, does the analysis package need any syntactic or semantic information about the word, etc? As a second example, the addition of new text may significantly alter the frequency of words in the data base and the manager may want to include more words in the common word list. It is interesting to note that the first of these examples, the introduction of a new word, involves only minor local changes to the data base, whilst in the second case, changing an existing word to a common word, involves retrospective changes to all references to that word.

As the text in the data base grows, so the data base manager should review and if necessary enhance the user aids available for searching the data base. The general outline of the user interface will have been decided at the design stage but minor changes may need to be made as the data base grows. In a menu driven system there may be a need to add items to existing menus or to add complete new menus in order to direct the user to new areas of the data base. If the interface is based on natural language then the changes in the linguistic analysis used for the main data base should sufficient to deal with any changes that are required in the user interface. Command driven systems should require little change to existing commands, indeed this should be discouraged on the grounds that it will cause confusion to existing users. It may, however, be necessary to introduce new commands to handle new text structures which have been added to the data base. If these new commands can be implemented using macros then this provides a simple method of trying out different commands, prompts and defaults before deciding on a definite form for the new command.

It is important that the facilities for data output keep in step with any new text structures that are added to the data base. This is particularly important in systems where a report generator is used — new proformas will have to be added as the structure of the text processing system grows. All these points are illustrated in the following example which looks at the building and development of the text processing system of the last example.

6.3.1 Example
Consider the text processing system of section 6.2.2. We have already outlined a possible design for the system, in this example we will look at some of the decisions the data base manager will have to make during the building of the data base. Let us look first at the input of text into the system. Three possible sources of information are:

(i) locally generated information on the ordering, stocks and cost of drugs
(ii) details of particular drugs available from manufacturers in the form of information sheets.
(iii) general pharmaceutical information extracted from the published literature.

The data from (i) may be available in machine readable form from a local computerised ordering system. In this case, the data base manager will have to design software to transform this data to the required format and verify the transformed data; since the data should already have been checked it will be sufficient to perform only random checks. It is unlikely that this data need be completely up to date; it would be sufficient to update it on a weekly basis.

The manufacturer's data (ii) will probably have to be typed directly into the system, preferably using a prompting program. If the manufacturers produce a new form of information sheet then the input procedures will have to be extended to cope with this. Since the text is likely to contain important technical information, the data base manager will probably decide to completely verify all this input. In view of the requirement to provide rapid identification of *all* drugs, once some new drug information has been added to the system and checked, the data base should be updated as soon as possible.

The general information (iii) may be gathered on an *ad hoc* basis. In all probability the data base manager would appoint one or more qualified people to abstract relevant material from the published literature and this could be checked and added into the system as and when there was time available.

In this particular system the common words and thesaurus terms would reflect the restricted subject matter of the source text. A medical dictionary could be used to provide some initial terms for the thesaurus but the need for other terms might only become apparent as the use of the system increased, e.g. the rapid identification of drugs may require the use of thesaurus terms to cover the physical description of tablets. Similar comments would apply to the choice of common words.

The data base manager will also have to consider two other items: the use of macros for searching and the use of proformas for report generation. As the data base grows, we can expect some pattern of use to begin to emerge. In this example certain types of searches for identification of drugs may become very common and so the data base manager should set up macros to help the user perform these types of searches quickly and efficiently. One such macro, for example, could prompt the user for size, shape and colour and produce a list of tablets that match that physical description. Similarly, the data base manager should set up general proformas for types of reports that are commonly required. □

In this section we have tried to emphasize the fact that a text processing system should be regarded as dynamic rather than static. Even though the user may have provided a very detailed set of requirements, his needs are likely to change with time. (They may even have changed by the time the system is installed and working.) The design should be sufficiently flexible to allow for such change and the data base manager should be prepared to devote considerable effort to building and modifying the data base.

6.4 DATA INTEGRITY

Once a text processing system has been built, though the original design meets the user requirements, the actual system might not perform as specified in the design with the result that the system does not meet the user requirements. One of the major problems in this area occurs when text, which has been entered into the system, is not stored correctly in the data base and cannot subsequently be retrieved. This is known as **data corruption**; in this section we will look at possible causes of data corruption, discuss what can be done to maintain the integrity of data in the system and see what methods are available to the data base manager to recover from a corrupted data base.

There are three main factors that can lead to data corruption. They are:

   (i) design — the design fails to handle certain (unexpected) combinations of input data
  (ii) software — the software of the text processing system does not correctly implement the original design
 (iii) operating system — the underlying operating system (and hardware) does not correctly support the text processing software.

The effect of data corruption can vary from trivial to very serious. We can define three levels of severity:

   (i) fatal — prevents the user from performing some required function, for example, corruption of a main menu in a browsing system

  (ii) serious — hinders the user in performing some required function, but some alternative method is available, for example, failure to add text to a given sction of the data base requiring the text to be added to another section

 (iii) minor — inconveniences the user in performing some required function, for example, incorrect forrr atting of text on display.

The data base manager should do all he can to reduce the possibility of all types of error. The design should be checked to ensure that it handles all possible data combinations, the software should be thoroughly tested to verify that it matches the design and lastly, though this is more relevant to the computer manager than the data base manager, the operating system and hardware should be well maintained. It will usually be impractical to check all possible text inputs against all possible states of the data base. As a result there may be some undiscovered design or implementation faults which could cause problems when the system is in a certain, untested, state. The possibility of this type of error can be reduced by keeping the data base in a tidy, well defined and well tested state. Thus, the system should provide the data base manager with a set of programs to tidy up the data base. In particular, the following functions will need to be performed:

   (i) garbage collection — to collect together any out of date information and clearly mark it as such

  (ii) extension/compression — to adjust the size of the data base, number of documents, size of documents etc to meet the current requirements

 (iii) integration — to re-order the data base to ensure that all new text is well integrated into the existing data base, for example, sorting sequential files, reclustering clustered files etc.

It is interesting to note that tidying up the data base may considerably improve the performance and efficiency of the system; this is often just as important as reducing the possibility of data corruption.

Once it is observed that the data base has been corrupted the data base manager must restore the data integrity. To do this he must either have some record of the recent state of the data base from which a valid version can be reconstructed, or else have some understanding of the internal structure of the data base which can be used to correct the corrupted data. So far we have said very little about the physical means used to store the text in a text processing system, but in order to understand the recovery techniques available, one needs to know a little about the physical storage mechanisms. The text, in both its original and analysed forms, will usually be stored in a number of files on a direct access storage device (exchangeable or fixed disk, drum etc). Each file will consist of a number of blocks of data together with some control information, such as cross-refernces to other files. Data corruption will lead to one or more of these blocks containing invalid data or control information. The aim of recovery techniques is to correct these blocks whilst leaving the rest of the data base as it is; since the error may affect just one block in ten or a hundred thousand blocks, recovery is far from trivial.

One of the simplest ways of maintaining data integrity is to keep a back-up copy of the data base. Errors are most likely to occur when the data base is being updated; so if all the updates can be batched together into a single job then we can make a copy of the data base just before it is updated. If an error is detected during or after the update we can revert to the original version of the data base, make the necessary corrections and re-run the data base update. Note that before this second update, just as before all others, the data base should be copied in case the update fails. It may be that a particular mistake is not discovered until some time later. To deal with this possibility one needs to keep a whole archive of copies of the data base. These copies can usually be made on magnetic tape — a fairly cheap and convenient means of storage, even so it would be impractical to keep a permanent copy of the data base before every update. One commonly used solution is to use a cycle of tapes. Thus if we have a set of five tapes we can copy the data base to a different tape at the end of each working day and cycle through the same sequence of tapes the following week. For added reliability we can maintain another cycle of four weekly tapes — at the end of each week the 'Friday' tape moves to the weekly cycle and its place in the daily cycle is taken by the oldest weekly tape. Similarly, we can have a cycle of twelve monthly tapes and finally copy the 'December' tape to an archive for permanent storage. Using this technique it is possible, with a small number of tapes, to recover the state of the data base as it was at the end of any day within the last week, or at the end of any week within the last month, or at the end of any month within the last year or at the end of any previous year. This is illustrated in Fig. 6.2. Though this method works well, it can be very time consuming to copy all of a large data base, especially if it does not all fit on a single magnetic tape. If the data base consists of a number of independent files then we can copy part of the data base each day and build up a valid version of the data base at the end of the week or month. Needless to say the penalty for this is that it may be necessary to go back several days to recover a valid version of the data base.

If the number of changes to the data base is small in relation to the total size of the data base, it may be easier to keep a copy of the changes rather than the data base itself. The principle is that a copy of the data base is taken at fairly infrequent intervals and in between, every change to the data base is recorded; so by starting off with an old copy of the data base and running

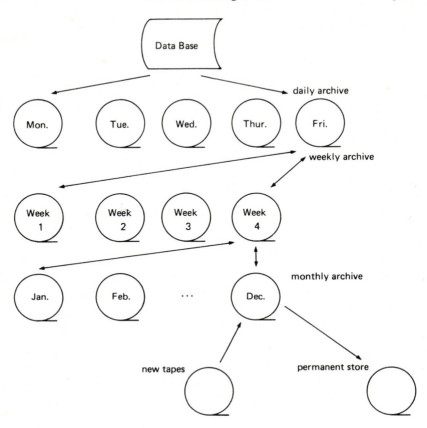

Fig. 6.2 – Archive tape cycle.

through all the changes we can recreate the state of the data base at any previous time. There are two stages at which we can store changes to the data base, either at the user input stage or else at the stage of writing physical blocks. In the former case, a log is kept of all transactions that would change the data base; to recover from an earlier copy of the data base these transactions are re-entered and the system updates the data base. In the latter case, as blocks containing new information are written to the data base a separate copy is kept of each changed block; the data base can then be restored by adding these blocks to a copy of the old version of the data base.

In the preceding discussion we have assumed that the data base manager has taken steps to record the previous states of the data base, and that return to an earlier state is a suitable recovery technique. This is certainly the simplest technique but it may be possible to use some knowledge of the system to recover from data corruption without resorting to back-up copies. For example, if one pointer to a text document in a data base is corrupted then it may be possible to recreate the pointer from other data in the system. This type of recovery can be performed either automatically or manually. The former case involves building a set of recovery programs, which have an implicit knowledge of the structure of the data base, to be used in the event of certain well defined error conditions. The latter case involves providing the data base manager with a set of general purpose tools for looking at and modifying the data base. One of the most useful functions these tools can perform is to allow the data base manager to look at any block in the data base and make any modifications to the data in that block. This is a very powerful facility but one which should be used only as a last resort; there is a great possibility of modifying the wrong bit of data out of the millions available.

Since all the data in any text processing system originated as plain text it should always be possible to recover that original text. In general the text will be stored in a simpler format than the analysed data and so is less likely to be corrupted. So even if the analysed data is totally corrupted, it should still be possible to extract the source text and use that to rebuild the data base. This facility can act as a final safeguard in the case of total data corruption, and it is also useful in transferring text from one system to another.

It is impossible to be sure that anything as complex as a text processing system will be free of errors. The data base manager should do all he can to reduce the possibility of errors but he must always be prepared to deal with any failures in the system. This requires regular maintenance of the data base and provision of data for recovery in the event of errors. For more details of recovery techniques the reader is referred to the survey of Verhofstad (1978).

6.5 DATA SECURITY

If a text processing system is being used by a number of people then some of those people may want to restrict access to data they have stored in the system. In a general multi-user environment the data base manager should provide some means of data security to ensure that sensitive information is available only to authorised users. An illustration of the need for such security can be found in the pharmaceutical data base discussed earlier in this chapter; it may prove more efficient to allow individual manufacturers access to the data base to add information on their new drugs, but the data base manager should not allow them access to information about the ordering of drugs from other manufacturers. In this case the disclosure of sensitive information could lead to one manufacturer having an unfair commercial advantage over its competitors; in other cases, such as criminal records, the effect of unauthorised disclosure could be more severe. A general discussion of the protection of information is given by Turn (1977). In the rest of this section we will look at some of the security methods that are available and discuss the protection they provide.

As with all security systems, the more inside information a person has about a text processing system the easier it is for him to gain unauthorised access to sensitive data. For example, if a person does not even know of the existence of a particular text processing system then he will not be able to gain access to it, whilst a programmer at the installation running the system may have sufficient knowledge to look at any text in the system. We can classify the methods of data security according to the knowledge required to overcome them. This may seem a rather negative attitude but it should be realised that in any computer installation there will be people who can access any data stored on that machine. This means it may be necessary in certain circumstances to physically restrict access to the computer installation, communications network and remote terminals.

We will consider first the case of a person authorised to use the system but not allowed to access all of the data base. We will assume that the user accesses the system by a remote on-line terminal, this will involve:

(i) connecting the terminal to the computer either by a private communications network or by the public telephone network

(ii) identifying yourself to the computer by means of some sign-on procedure

(iii) authenticating your identification

(iv) requesting access to the text processing system.

The information required to perform each of these steps can be restricted but in practice it is the third stage, authentication, which is used to control access to the system. A number of methods are available:

(i) supplying a personal password

(ii) performing a personal calculation on some computer generated data

(iii) reading a coded magnetic card

(iv) voice recognition.

These last two methods involve extra equipment at the user's terminal; this reflects a general principle that it will cost money to provide an effective security system. Once the user has successfully gone through the above procedures, he is connected to the text processing system and the system will recognise him by the identification provided at step (ii) in the access sequence — this is usually a short character string called the user identification code (UIC). It is now up to the text processing system to decide what data this user should be allowed to access.

To maintain data security there will be certain actions on certain data that the data base manager will want to restrict to a given group of authorised users. For any given document the user may want to:

(i) read the document

(ii) add some text to the document

(iii) change parts of the document

(iv) destroy the document

The simplest approach says that if a user is authorised to do just one of these actions then he is authorised to do them all; at the other extreme the user will require separate permission to perform each action. For the rest of this section we will consider the case of two types of action:

(i) Read – read the document

(ii) Write – add, change or destroy the document.

In addition we shall assume that if a user is authorised to write a document he is automatically authorised to read it. Now for each user there will be a set of documents that he can read, and this can be represented in a (Venn) diagram as in Fig. 6.3. Suppose there are three users $U1$, $U2$ and $U3$ – the documents to which each has access can overlap in a number of ways. Some of the possibilities are illustrated in Fig. 6.4. In (a) there is a linear hierarchy of access. This can be provided by giving each user a numeric access key and allowing a user to access a document if and only if its access key is less than or equal to that of the user. This simple approach will not work for the second case (b) where the documents are arranged in a tree structure. If the nodes of the tree are labelled, then by assigning the relevant labels to each document and user, we can allow the user access to

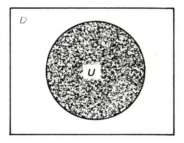

Fig. 6.3 – Single user read access.

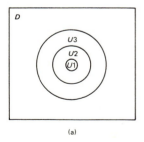

(a)

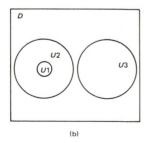

(b)

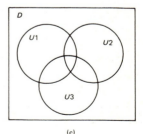

(c)

Fig. 6.4 – Multiple user read access.

just those documents in his own subtree. So in this example user $U2$ would have the code 1 to indicate that he could see only those documents whose code began with 1, user $U1$ would have the code 1.1 and could see documents beginning with 1.1, and user $U3$ would have the code 2. The final case (c) represents the most general possibility — here each document must contain a list of those users authorised to see the document. This could be stored as a list of user identification codes or else as a binary string where a 1 or 0 in positon i indicates that user U_i does or does not have access to the document.

Though this model can cope with many situations it has certain limitations. We have assumed that for a given user, or group of users, certain data either is or is not available. This is only true if the information is context free, that is, the sensitivity of any information in the text processing system is independent of any other information the user may have; this is not always so. Consider the statistics produced as a result of a national census; since all names and addresses are removed one would suspect that the data could be freely available. If, however, a person had access to a list of names and addresses (for example, the electoral register) then for any small area it might be possible to correlate the individual statistical data with the list of names and addresses and so obtain confidential information about named individuals. In this case we say that the information is **context sensitive** and some more powerful means of data security is required. The solution that has been adopted to deal with the census problem is to introduce random variations into the small area statistics — this does not affect the use of the data for statistical purposes but makes it impossible to identify individual data items. A discussion of the general problem can be found in Hassiao and Baum (1976).

The data base manager may have to consider the security of the data, not only with respect to the end user, but also with respect to the system programmer. If there is a need for new software to meet ad-hoc user requirements then the system programmer will need access to the data base to develop and test his programs. So the system will have to check that the programs themselves are authorised to access the data base. Similar techniques to those discussed above can be used, but it is important to point out that any authentication of the user identifier should be left until run-time rather than incorporated in the program code. A detailed description of one particular approach, the CODASYL approach, to this side of data security is given by Olle (1978) in his Chapter 18.

The security measures that we have discussed so far have been aimed at allowing authorised use of the text processing system to access parts of a data base. But there will be other methods of accessing the information in the data base and in sensitive areas further methods must be taken to prevent unauthorised access. For example, a system programmer with knowledge of the names and structures of the data base files could write a program to print a copy of the whole data base and so extract sensitive information; this can be overcome by encrypting the text stored on the computer files. Similarly, a communications engineer could tap the lines connecting a remote terminal to the computer and monitor the information flowing between the user and data base; once again this can be overcome by encrypting the data that is being transmitted. Various methods of data encryption are possible, and one very secure method currently in use is **public key encryption.** This uses a pair of inverse function encode (e) and decode (d) such that given the function d it is easy to calculate the function e, but given e it is practically impossible to calculate d. The user chooses such a function d, computes the function e and gives it to the text processing system. The system can then use e to store the user's data in an encrypted form but only the user will be able to decode it. Such a scheme is described in more detail by Ingemarsson and Wong (1981).

The need for data security is growing with the increasing number of computerised information systems. The data base manager should be aware from the start, of the problems of storing sensitive, or potentially sensitive, information in a text processing system.

6.6 USER SUPPORT

We discussed in section 5.6 some of the user aids that can be incorporated into a text processing system; although these are necessary it is unlikely that they will be sufficient for all users and therefore the data base manager will have to provide additional user support. The areas where this is most important are:

 (i) Training – to introduce new users to the system
 (ii) Back up – to give additional support not provided by the on-line user aids.
 (iii) Problem reporting – to provide a method for reporting and correcting problems in the text processing system.

Though the users may be familiar with the overall aims of the system they may need instruction on how to use it efficiently in order to satisfy their particular requirements. This can best be met by a program of training courses, demonstrations and supervised practical experience in using the system. This training needs to be supported by printed guides and full documentation of the user interface. Even after such a training program the user may still encounter difficulties with the system and some continuing back up support will be required. Often the user will want the system to perform some function not specified in the original design; this may not be feasible and will he need help in deciding on the best course of action.

Finally, it is important to realise that errors will occur within the software and the data base of the text processing system. There must be procedures for a user to inform the data base manager of any errors he has encountered. The manager can then take the following action.

   (i) acknowledge the existence of the problem
  (ii) identify the nature of the problem
 (iii) implement short and long term fixes
 (iv) inform the user of these corrections.

As an example of (iii), if the user found two copies of the same document in a data base then the short term fix would be to remove one copy while the long term fix would be to look at the input procedures and add checks to detect multiple copies.

6.7 SUMMARY

It would be ideal if each user were in complete control of his own text processing system, but this is possible only in a small single-user environment. As the system grows the user will need help in understanding it and making the best possible use of its facilities. As the data base grows more effort will have to be spent on maintaining the validity and integrity of the text. And, as the number of users increase one must ensure that they do not interfere with each other's use of the system. In this chapter we have showed how these functions can be performed by a data base manager and discussed some of the principles involved. The most important of these principles is that a text processing system is more than a piece of software for analysing and storing text, it is a tool which must be well built and well maintained if it is to perform its intended function. The algorithms used to analyse, store and retrieve the text will only be a part of the whole system and hence cannot be used efficiently unless the rest of the system is properly managed. The data base manager should be involved in all aspects of the system, from the initial design and building of the data base, through the preparation of user aids to the reliability of the system and the addition of new facilities.

   We have now discussed all the major components of a text processing system, the analysis and storage of the text, the means of extracting information from the data base, the user's interface with the data base and the overall management of the system. In the next chapter we shall see how these can be integrated into a working system.

7

Integrated Systems

Observe how system into system runs,
What other planets circle other suns.

Alexander Pope
An Essay on Man

7.1 INTRODUCTION

There is a great diversity in the range of applications in which text processing systems can be used. Throughout this book we have given various isolated examples and, by now, the reader should be able to supply many more from his own experience. There is a similar diversity in the number of algorithms that can be used in building a text processing system, though we have been able to look at only the most important. It seems then, that there is a very large number of possible systems to handle all the different applications. This is already apparent with many large companies and institutions supporting several different information systems, for example, personnel, stock control, invoicing, library management etc. Within the organisation a single user may, for a single job, require access to several different data bases: for example, library staff may have to check the personnel data base before adding a new reader to the list of library users. Similarly the user may require access to several different systems to produce a particular product. For example, the printing of a current awareness list will require four separate processes:

    (i) extract the documents from the data base
    (ii) sort the documents into subject and author order
    (iii) edit the documents to the required format
    (iv) typeset and print the documents.

and each of these processes could well be a separate system. One can very easily build up complex networks of data bases and systems as shown in Fig. 7.1. One possible method of reducing the complexity of this multi-user multi-system environment is to produce a single monolithic system as in Fig. 7.2. But even if it is possible to produce such a system, all it has done is to replace a

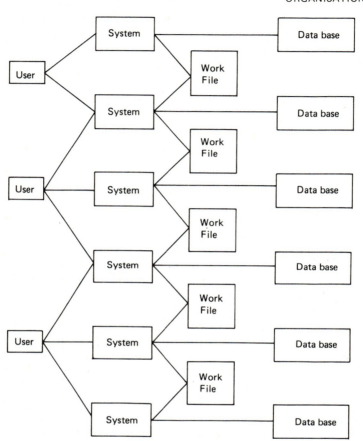

Fig. 7.1 — Multi-user multi-system environment.

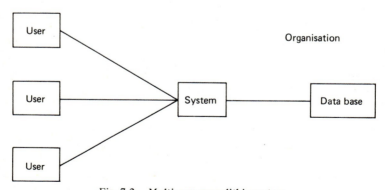

Fig. 7.2 — Multi-user monolithic system.

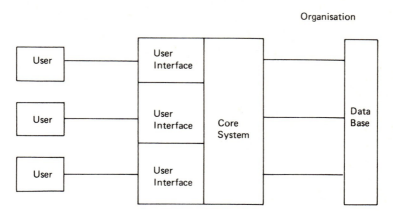

Fig. 7.3 — Multi-user integrated system.

complex network by an equally complex monolithic system. In all probability such a system will be difficult to maintain and almost impossible to modify. An intermediate approach can be developed based on a single core system with a number of user interfaces — one for each application. This type of integrated system can be represented as in Fig. 7.3.

The principle of developing a general purpose system to meet a number of different applications is common in other areas of computing. One does not have to build special purpose hardware for every user application, one can use standard hardware and, if necessary, tailor it to each particular application. One does not need to design a new programming language for every new application, one language can serve many applications. Similarly, one does not need to design special systems for every application, it is often possible to integrate different systems into a single framework. In the rest of this chapter we shall see how this principle can be applied to text processing systems.

7.2 SOFTWARE PACKAGES

When a data base manager comes to set up a new information system there is often a tendency for him to regard his particular application as unique and requiring specially written software. It has long been realised that many different applications can be supported on the same hardware using the same programming language; indeed the present level of computerisation would not have been possible without the introduction of general purpose hardware and high level languages. Any further increase in the level of computerisation will require taking this principle a stage further with the development and use of general purpose software packages. The aim of a software package should be to produce a single system which meets as many of the requirements as possible for as many applications as possible. It is often difficult to see the common ground in the existing diversity of user applications; a good software package should identify the common ground and build on it. Naturally, any one package will not be suitable for all applications in its particular field, and any one application may require some specially written software to meet the needs of its own users. As a general rule, in each application the package should account for at least 80% of the total software, leaving at most 20% to be written; if the application requires much more specially written software than the chances are that the chosen software package is not well suited to the task in hand.

The use of a software package has a number of advantages. Some of the more important are:

(i) reduction in the amount of programming required
(ii) use of a tried, tested and documented system
(iii) availability of established maintenance procedures
(iv) support of a user community.

It is reassuring to know that many of the problems associated with new software will have been overcome in an established package. In addition, the fact that the package already exists means that it is possible to evaluate the proposed system in detail without embarking on any expensive software development. The maintenance of large programs is always a problem but in the case of a software package, the supplier should have established procedures for reporting and correcting errors in the system. Finally, it is often helpful to be able to exchange ideas and comments within a group of people who are using the same software package for similar applications.

Despite the advantages of using software packages, a substantial number of organisations are using text processing systems that have been developed in-house. Ashford and Matkin (1980) have estimated that about two-thirds of the users of data base systems have developed their own software. It is worthwhile listing some of the possible reasons for this:

(i) suitable packages were not available at the right time
(ii) suitable packages were available but were not seen to be suitable
(iii) suitable packages were available but were not known about
(iv) users wanted to write their own system (for reasons of research, prestige, and 'not invented here' syndrome, etc.
(v) management wanted their own system (for reasons of politics, finance, accounting etc).

There are now a number of text processing/information retrieval packages available, (see Appendix I). To give some idea of the range of facilities available we shall describe one of these systems, STATUS, in some detail. As with the other packages, the facilities that are available will change from time to time, and for up to date information the reader is referred to the vendor of the software package.

7.3 STATUS TEXT STRUCTURE

We shall consider the structures used for storing text in STATUS from the three viewpoints — user, system and physical — set out in section 3.1.

From the user's point of view, the basic unit of information storage is the **article**. At its simplest this is just a piece of text of arbitrary length — it could be a bibliographic reference, a personnel record, a technical report, etc. The **article** is the standard unit for input and output of text, and corresponds to a **document**, as defined in section 3.2 The delimiter **££T** is used to introduce a new article and **££A** to end it. There is additional structure both above and below the article level.

Within each article the text can be divided up into a number of sections. These sections are given user defined names, and are referred to as **named sections**. These **named sections** correspond to the **field** as defined in section 4.4 (v), like articles they can be of arbitrary length. The sections are identified by tag lines of the form

> **££N** section name

So, for example, the articles containing bibliographic references could have named sections called **AUTHOR, TITLE, PUBLISHER** etc, while the personnel records could have **NAME, ADDRESS, JOB** etc. At the lowest level the named section consists of a sequence of words. In the STATUS system a word is defined as a sequence of user defined, concordable characters terminated by any other, non-concordable, character (as in section 2.2.1). So if the concordable characters were

> A, B, , , , Z, 0, 1, . . . 9, -, #

then the following would be valid STATUS words:

> WORD, WORD1, CO-OP, 123 #123

We have seen (section 4.4) that Boolean search functions distinguish only between the presence or absence of a word. In order to allow numeric range searching, STATUS has extended the definition of a word to allow certain words to have an associated value. This combination is called a **key field** and consists of a key field name and an associated key field value. Key fields are identified by the # (hash) symbol so

> #HEIGHT 1.92

is a key field whose name is HEIGHT and whose associated value is 1.92.

The article has some more structure in addition to the named sections and key fields. The text at the beginning of the article, from the initial **££T** up to a matching **££T**, forms a short title and is used for identifying the article. The text within named sections can be divided up into unnamed sections, or paragraphs; these are delimited by **££P**.

Within a STATUS system, articles are grouped together to form data bases. A STATUS data base is a self-contained set of articles covering some particular user application. For example all the bibliographic references for a library could be grouped together to form a data base, similarly all the personnel records for an organisation. All the articles in one data base must have a similar structure. In particular, for each data base the data base manager must set up the following parameters to define the structure of the data base and its articles:

(i)   the maximum size for any article
(ii) the list of available section names
(iii) the set of concordable characters and key field names
(iv) the list of users who are authorised to access the data base.

With any data base there is the ability to group articles into chapters. Generally, related articles are grouped into a single chapter, for example all the technical reports for a given year could form a chapter within the main data base. The chapter structure can be used to limit the scope of any subsequent data base searches; it also serves to partition large data bases into smaller sections.

The text structure incorporates a linear hierachy of access as described in section 6.5. A user may be denied access to particular data bases, chapters within a data base, articles and even named sections. Wherever possible, the system acts as though the text did not exist rather than that the user was not allowed to see it. So if the user asks to select a particular data base, the system response is exactly the same whether the data base does not exist or whether it does exist but the user is not authorised to see it. Thus sensitive information is not only kept secure, but its very existence is kept secret. The user's view of the text is summarised in Fig. 7.4.

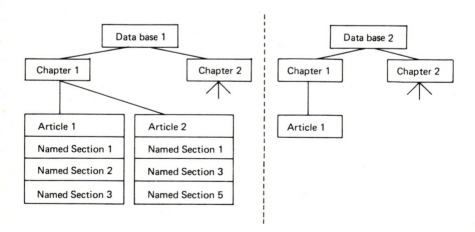

Fig. 7.4 – STATUS text structure – user's view.

From the system point of view, the text is stored in chains of fixed length records, These records have an index structure that reflects the user view of the data, as is shown in Fig. 7.5. The use of chained sequences of fixed length records allows for the efficient storage of variable numbers of variable length articles. For example in Fig. 7.5, article 1, of Chapter 1, is shown as a chain of two records, if the user wanted to add more text to this article then this can be achieved by adding more records onto the chain. From the preceding discussion of the user view it should be apparent that, for each data base, the system must maintain a list of available section names, the set of concordable characters and a list of authorised users. These lists are also stored in chains of fixed length records, the special block contains pointers to the head of each chain.

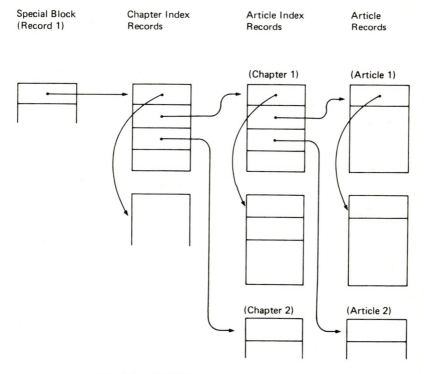

Fig. 7.5 – STATUS text structure – system view.

At the physical level the text will be held as data blocks on a storage medium such as fixed disc. On some hardware it may be more economical to store many logical records in one physical block. (This is similar to storing many catalogue cards in one drawer of a card cabinet, and causes similar problems if two people want to use the same drawer at the same time). In addition, the amount of disc transfer may be reduced if the system keeps, in main memory, a copy of the most recently used blocks. These techniques can save a considerable amount of disc storage space and disc I/O time; however, they cause problems in a multi-user environment. For reading records it is necessary to ensure that the in-core copy is up to date, since a second user may have changed the record without the knowledge of the first user. Even more care is necessary when writing to a record. Firstly, to change a record in a block it is necessary to read the whole block, modify the required record and re-write the whole block. If two users attempt to write different records in the same physical block then one user's modifications could get overwritten by the other. This is illustrated in Fig. 7.6.

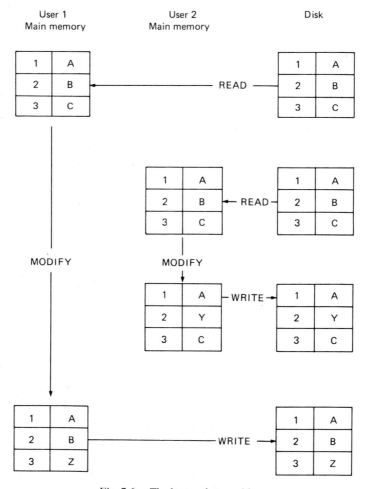

Fig. 7.6 – The lost update problem.

So to write a record, it is necessary to perform the following steps:

(i) lock the file to prevent other users writing to it
(ii) read in the block containing the record to be modified
(iii) modify the record
(iv) re-write the block
(v) unlock the file.

7.4 BASIC STATUS FUNCTIONS

The STATUS system provides a means of storing, modifying and retrieving textual information. In the previous section we saw how text is stored in the system, in this section we shall look at some of the basic methods of modifying and retrieving the text. The retieval capability is based on the Boolean search functions (see section 4.4.1) with a command driven user interface (see section 5.4). The syntax of the commands is given in Fig. 7.7. It should be noted that questions such as

Q (information + processing) // textual?

are syntactically invalid, since the result of the AND (+) operator is an article reference list and this can not be an operand for the collection (//) operator.

search command ::= Q $<$*article ref*$>$*?*
article ref ::= ($<$ article ref $>$)
          $<$*article ref*$>$, $<$*article ref*$>$ logical OR
          $<$*article ref*$>$ + $<$*article ref*$>$ logical AND
          $<$*article ref*$>$ -- $<$*article ref*$>$ logical NOT
          $<$*word ref*$>$ basic membership function
          $<$*word ref*$>$ @ $<$*named section spec*$>$ field search
named section spec ::= $<$*named section list*$>$
          (ALL – $<$*named section list*$>$)
named section list   ::= $<$*named section*$>$
          ($<$*named section*$>$, $<$*named section list*$>$)
word ref ::=   ($<$*word ref*$>$)
          $<$*word ref*$>$, $<$*word ref*$>$ logical OR
          $<$*word ref*$>$/m, n/$<$*word ref*$>$ collocation
          $<$*word ref*$>$ $<$*word ref*$>$ phrase, implied collocation
          $<$*word*$>$ basic membership function
          $<$*word*$>$*   truncation

Fig. 7.7 – STATUS question syntax.

In the previous section we saw that STATUS had introduced the concept of key fields - words with essential numeric values. This means that it is possible to search for numerical values in a particular range. The definition of a word reference in Fig. 7.7 can be extended to include:

$$
\begin{aligned}
\text{Key field name} \quad &< \quad \text{value} \\
&= \quad \text{value} \\
&> \quad \text{value} \\
&>< \quad \text{value 1} \quad \text{value 2}
\end{aligned}
$$

The final form indicates searching for key field values greater than value 1 but less than value 2.

7.4.1 Example
The following are valid STATUS questions:

(i) **Q information?**	simple search for all articles containing the word **information**.
(ii) **Q information processing ?**	phrase, or implied collocation search for all article containing the phrase **information processing**
(iii) **Q (information processing) @ title ?**	as (ii) but restricted to **title** section
(iv) **Q (information processing) @ title ?** **+ # publish > 1980?**	as (iii) but restricted to those with year of publication after 1980. ▫

The result of a STATUS question is to set up a list of articles which satisfy the question. This is called the **retrieved list** and is central to subsequent commands. When a user has a valid retrieved list he has the following options:

(i) look at some or all of the articles on the list
(ii) issue further commands to refine the search and reduce the number of articles on the list
(iii) ignore the existing list and ask a new question to generate a new retrieved list.

There are two commands that can be used to refine the search. The first is the **SUBQ** command, which acts just like the **Q** (question) command except that it applies only to articles on the current retrieved list. The second command is **SCAN**. This command performs a sequential scan through the text of all the articles on the retrieved list and finds those articles containing text which matches that given in the **SCAN** command. Note that although the truncation operator acts only on the right hand end of words, it is possible to perform left hand, and general, truncation using the **SCAN** command.

There are a number of commands available for displaying the text of the retrieved articles. The basic form of these commands is:

$$< \text{display command} > \quad < \text{route} > \quad < \text{article specification} >$$

The display command is one of the following:

D	display the whole article
DS	display specified named sections
DSI	display specified named sections in internal format
DP	display specified paragraphs
STRING	display text following a given character string.

The route parameter is optional; if present it specifies the destination for the output. The default is the terminal, but it is also possible to route text to a fast printer or to temporary or permanent files. The article specification parameter is also optional, and is used to indicate which articles on the retrieved list are to be processed. The default is that the command applies to the current article; the current article is the last article that was displayed or, if no articles from the retrieved list have been displayed, then the current article is the first article on the retrieved list.

7.4.2 Example
The following are valid STATUS display commands:

(i)	**D**	display the current article
(ii)	**DS TITLE**	display the title section of the current article
(iii)	**DS TITLE 1-5**	display the title section of the first five articles
(iv)	**DS PRINT TITLE 1-5**	as (iii) but send the output to the printer. □

As well as looking at the text of retrieved documents it is possible to browse through the data base looking at each article in turn. If individual articles are very long then, on display, the text is divided into a number of pages and it is possible to browse through the pages of individual articles. Finally, there is a command, **ZOOM**, which will scan through the text of long articles and display those pages containing a given text string. These features allow the user to browse rapidly through large volumes of text.

To complete the description of the basic functions, we shall describe how a STATUS user can extend and modify his data base. At their simplest these two functions are very similar, each requiring three steps:

(i) obtain the article − for adding new articles to the data base this in-involves typing in the text of the new article (using the **ADD** command), for modifying an existing article it involves locating the article either by browsing or asking a question;

(ii) edit the article — to correct any mistakes made in typing in the new article or to make the required modifications to the old article;

(iii) update — to incorporate the new material in the data base.

STATUS provides its own editor; it is a simple contextual editor (see section 5.3 (ii)). As well as the advantages that were outlined in section 5.3, the use of an integrated editor allows the user to restrict the scope of the contextual editing to a given named section. At the end of stage (ii), above, the text is automatically checked for STATUS syntax errors. Any errors can either be corrected automatically using a set of standard fix-up rules, or else the user can return to the editor and manually correct the text. Once the text is accepted it is stored with other new material on a list of pending changes called the **amendment list**. Finally, the data base manager can, at any time, issue the **UPDATE** command to take all the material on the amendment list and incorporate it in the data base. Note that it is only at the update stage that it is possible to check the text for the existence of new words; so to correct any spelling or other mistakes detected as a result of this vocabulary logging a second edit and update cycle is required.

The system implementation of these basic functions follows fairly closely the standard algorithms that we have already described. The search questions are implemented using a version of the algorithm in section 4.4.3. The dictionary structure is similar to that in algorithm 3.4.6; the main difference is that the index at each level is to pairs of letters (digraphs or digrams) rather than to individual letters. The second level digraph index is usually fairly sparse and so it is stored as a list of actual digraphs with their associated pointers. In order to support full positional searching, the reference lists give the complete word reference — chapter, article, paragraph and word number — of every occurrence of each word. The index is stored, like the text, in a file of linked, fixed length records called the concordance file. The structure of the concordance file is shown in Fig. 7.8. Note that those words which are key field names have a special reference list which contains not only all the 4-level references but also the key field value associated with each occurrence of the key field name.

7.5 ADVANCED STATUS FEATURES

The STATUS functions that we have described so far allow the user to store and retrieve a wide range of textual material. In addition, the system provides a number of other functions whose aim is to improve the user interface for text input, searching and data output. In general these advanced functions will require some initial effort from the data base manager to set them up for the individual user's requirements. Once they have been set up for a particular group of users they can then be used by all the members of the group without further intervention. The STATUS package offers, at present, the following features as optional extras.:

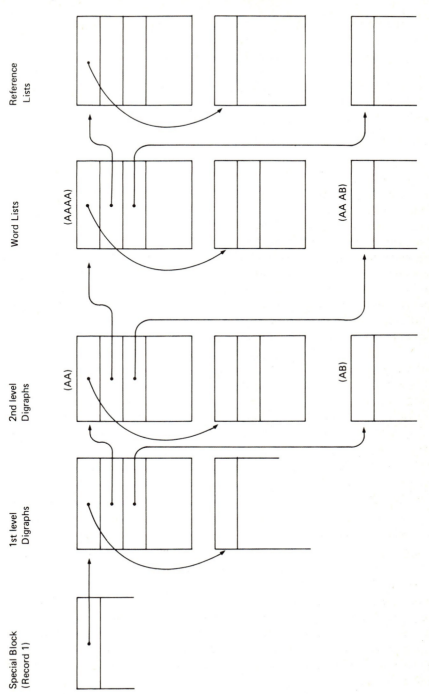

Fig. 7.8 – STATUS concordance file – system view.

(i)	SDPA	–	STATUS data preparation aid, a prompting program for text input
(ii)	Macros	–	a facility for the data base manager, or user, to store sequences of commands
(iii)	Thesaurus	–	a facility for storing thesaurus terms for use as a searching aid.
(iv)	REPGEN	–	A report generator for STATUS output.

We shall consider each of these in turn.

7.5.1 SDPA

Many computer manufacturers provide software to ease the burden of data preparation. But, as we saw in the case of editors, there are advantages in providing a data preparation aid that can be integrated with the rest of the text processing system. STATUS provides a line by line prompting program which is similar to that described in the algorithm of section 5.2.1. Since the data preparation aid has been designed to be used for generating STATUS input, a number of improvements are possible on the general design. A STATUS article can be regarded as lines of user text separated by system makers to indicate paragraphs, sections etc. This is reflected in SDPA in a number of ways.

Firstly, SDPA has special facilities to handle STATUS system markers. The proforma, or mask file accepts lines of the form

$$< \text{STATUS system marker} > \ < \text{prompt} > \ \textbf{NULL}$$

This prompts the user for text and then outputs the user text preceded by the system marker. The keyword **NULL** is optional, its presence signifies that if the user does not enter any text then the system marker itself should not be output. The prompt parameter is also optional; if it is omitted then a standard prompt is generated according to the type of the system marker.

Secondly, it is possible to link the system closely with the target data base. This allows the input to be checked more thoroughly than would otherwise be the case. For example a general purpose data preparation aid would know nothing about valid STATUS section names and so could not validate them, but this is possible if the data preparation aid is integrated with the rest of the text processing system.

Finally, many of the details of STATUS text structure can be handled more easily in SDPA than would be possible using a more general package. In particular, SDPA can simplify the layout and format control of STATUS articles.

7.5.2 Macros

Frequently parts of commands or command sequences may be common to many user requirements. This may be because of the particular nature and content of a data base or because particular patterns of usage have developed. The STATUS macro facility removes the need for typing such commands in full each time they are used, and provides a means of sharing such commands within a group of users. The principles behind the use of macros should be clear from the discussion in section 4.5. In STATUS, partial or complete commands may be stored as macros, given unique names and simply referred to by name within any valid command or other macro. The macro can contain dummy parameters which are replaced by actual parameters supplied by the user each time the macro is called. For parametered macros it is possible to assign to each parameter not only a default value and prompt but also a parameter type which can be used to validate the actual parameter supplied by the user. So, for example, a macro can specify that a particular parameter is going to be used as a named section specification and if the user supplies an invalid specification then it will be rejected immediately and the user given the chance to re-enter a valid specification; without this facility the error would not be detected until the macro had started to execute and recovery would be more difficult. This is an example of the benefits that are available from integrating the macro processor within the system rather than using a stand alone one. The STATUS macro facility does not support keyword parameters, as in the algorithm of section 5.4.1. However, if a parameter has no associated prompt then it is regarded as optional, and, unless the user supplies a value, the default value is used.

One novel feature of the STATUS macro processor is the treatment of informative, warning and error messages from the main system. There are two major problems when using macros involving a long sequence of commands:

(i) it may be difficult to relate standard system messages to the parameters given in the macro call

(ii) it may be desirable, in the event of certain errors, to stop the macro execution and invoke some other macro command.

These problems have been solved by the use of a macro conditional option. Each macro may have a list of warning and error conditions and associated actions. If an error occurs then the associated action is performed (cf. PL/I ON-codes). There are three possible types of action:

(i) suppress the error/warning messages and continue macro execution

(ii) output a macro specific message (which may contain macro parameters) and continue execution

(iii) suppress the message, stop the current macro execution and execute the associated command or macro.

With a little ingenuity it is possible to use this facility to completely change the STATUS interface to meet a variety of user applications (Wilson *et al.* 1981).

7.5.3 Thesaurus

When searching a data base a user may want to insert into his question a predefined list of words as an addition to a particular word he has thought of. This can be used to increase the recall of a search as we saw in section 4.4.

In the field of information retrieval, thesauri have principally been used for indexing documents prior to searching; the STATUS, free text, approach is to use a thesaurus not only for indexing, but also as a search aid. A STATUS thesaurus consists of a hierarchy of synonyms rings containing words used in the data base. If a user wants to search for articles dealing with a particular topic he can examine the thesaurus to find all the words in the data base that are used to describe that topic and include them in his search. The inclusion of these thesaurus terms can be either automatic or under user control. In the first case, if any word in a question is followed by the synonym expansion character '&' (ampersand) then all the synonyms for that word are automatically included in the search request. In the second case, the user can browse through the thesaurus and identify words he wants to include; these synonyms are then sorted in a macro and can be used in any subsequent search. In its present implementation, the STATUS thesaurus supports a general hierarchy of broader terms, narrower terms and head terms as well as related terms, see also terms and scope notes. It should be emphasised that when the thesaurus is being used as a search aid rather than as an indexing tool the concept of preferred term has no significance; each term in a synonym ring is equally likely to occur in any relevant article and so it is necessary to search for them all rather than one preferred term.

7.5.4 REPGEN

STATUS provides a report generator package, REPGEN, which enables the user to define the layout of a report containing any material that has been extracted from the data base. The first step in setting up a report is to identify the various items of data that are to be extracted from the data base. The required data may be a named section, paragraph, key field value or any string of text which is preceded by some unique tag. Once the user knows what data he wants to extract, he can set up a sequence of STATUS commands to search the data base and extract the required information. The commands can be stored either in a macro or in a file for use in batch mode. The STATUS facility for routing text enables the retrieved data to be stored in a temporary file, known as the transfer file, for input to the main REPGEN program.

To produce a report REPGEN requires three files, the transfer file, the proforma file and the command file. The transfer file, as we have seen, contains the raw data extracted from the data base. The proforma file contains the report proforma; this is similar to that in section 5.5.2, the main difference being that the slots for the extracted data are unlabelled and do not contain the data extraction commands. The command file contains a list of commands which specify how the data in the transfer file is to be inserted in the slots in the proforma. REPGEN maintains a number of registers which can be used to store numerical data, and algorithms are provided to perform various arithmetic operations on the values stored in these registers. The general form of a REPGEN command is

$$< \text{source data} > \; < \text{operation} > \; < \text{register} >$$

The source data can indicate either a word or group of words in the current line of the transfer file, or else a register which already contains data. The operation is either one of a set of standard operations (such as **store, output, add** etc) or else one of a number of user defined algorithms. The register parameter is required by some operations for the storage of numeric data. As the command file is processed, each item of data is read sequentially from the transfer file and the output data is placed, in order, in the slots in the proforma.

Setting up a report requires considerable skill. The STATUS command file, the REPGEN command file and the proforma must always be kept in step so that each data item extracted from the data base is processed by the correct REPGEN command and output to the right slot in the proforma. As with command macros, once the system has been set up then it is very easy to run.

7.6 MANAGEMENT OF STATUS DATA BASES

The STATUS data base manager has two sets of tools available to him for maintaining his data base. The first consists of a set of privileged commands in the main STATUS program. These commands are available only to data base managers and are concerned mainly with adding and deleting source text, permanent macros and thesaurus terms. The second set of tools comprise a number of stand alone utilities to perform various data management functions.

From the manager's point of view adding or deleting text is a two stage process. Firstly, authorised users put their prospective changes on the amendment list, as we saw in section 7.4. Secondly the data base manager checks the material on the amendment list and updates the data base. The manager has a set of privileged commands which allow him to:

(i) look at any article on the amendment list
(ii) make further changes to any article on the amendment list
(iii) remove any article from the amendment list.

Thus the manager can vet all prospective changes to the data base and allow only those which meet his approval. In addition to dealing with amendments entered by the users on-line, the data base manager has a facility for adding text in batch mode. For small amounts of text this can proceed in parallel with normal use of the data base, but for large amounts of text it is more efficient to use a special utility program which demands exclusive use of the data base.

Each user has the ability to define his own personal macros, but in addition to this the data base manager can set up a library of macros for each data base.

The personal macros are available only to the user who created them and, in some implementations, may be deleted at the end of a STATUS session. The data base macros, on the other hand, are always available to all users of the data base. The data base manager has commands available to store, rename and delete macros and can use these to maintain a library of macros to meet his user requirements.

In the present implementation, the STATUS thesaurus is built and maintained on-line by the data base manager using a set of privileged commands. From the description in section 7.5.3 it should be clear that there are two functions involved in building a thesaurus:

    (i) create sets of words which are to be regarded as synonyms (synonym rings)
    (ii) link these synonym rings into a hierarchy.

These functions are implemented using two commands:

    JOIN
    W_1 W_2 W_3

which creates a synonym ring containing the words W_1, W_2 and W_3, and

    TIE s_1 $<$ relation $>$ s_2

which links two synonym rings s_1 and s_2 by the specified relation — **BT** (broader term), **NT** (narrower term) etc. The synonym rings are identified either by reference to a previous display of synonyms or else by one of the words in the ring. A similar command **UNTIE** is available to remove a relation.

It would be impracticable to describe in detail all the utilities that are available for managing a STATUS data base. We shall restrict ourselves to looking at groups of utilities for performing the more important functions. The first group of utilities that we will consider is concerned with creating the data base. Before any text can be entered into a data base the data base must first be initialised. This involves:

    (i) allocating and formatting the disc space for storing the data base;
    (ii) setting up the parameters for the data base.

The parameters to be set up include:

    (i) data base title
    (ii) list of authorised users
    (iii) set of concordable characters
    (iv) set of common words
    (v) list of valid section names
    (vi) specification of key fields

Even after the data base has been created many of these parameters can be altered. In particular there are utilities to:

(i)   extend the size of the data base
(ii) compress unused space in the data base
(iii) alter the data base title
(iv) add new common words
(v)   add new section names

Authorising new users and specifying new key fields are performed by privileged commands in the main program. It is not possible to alter the set of concordable characters or to remove a word from the common word list as this would affect the whole data base. There are utilities to monitor the size of the data base and the vocabulary of the source text; these can be used to help the manager decide what changes are necessary.

Finally, STATUS provides facilities to help maintain the data integrity. There are two utilities to keep the data base in a tidy standard form:

(i) garbage collection — to check that all free records are correctly chained;
(ii) re-ordering — to group together related records into a single physical block.

It is assumed that standard operating system dump and restore facilities will be available and so these are not provided in the STATUS system. There are, however, utilities to help correct any data corruption. In particular the system can:

(i)   remove any records that appear to be invalid;
(ii) output all the original source text;
(iii) allow the manager to manually inspect and alter any data base record.

7.7 STATUS DISTRIBUTION SYSTEM

The commercial exploitation of any software package will require an efficient method of distribution. Even when a text processing system is running successfully on one machine it is not trivial to transfer it to another similar machine. When it is necessary to implement the system on a number of different machines of different types the problems become more acute. Finally, trying to maintain such a variety of implementations can prove a major problem. These problems are common to all organisations marketing software packages, and the only solution is to develop an efficient distribution system. For each new customer the STATUS distribution system carries out the following actions:

(i) identify the customer's requirements — system options, type of hardware, etc;
(ii) generate magnetic tape for required system implementation;

(iii) dispatch distribution kit — magnetic tape, installation manual, etc;
(iv) acknowledge receipt of any problems and pass on the relevant expert;
(v) keep the user informed of current action on problems affecting his installation;
(vi) dispatch system modifications.

In general each installation will support several different data bases each with their own data base manager. In this situation it is desirable to have an installation manager who is responsible for receiving and implementing the distribution kit and any subsequent system modifications. The STATUS package provides a number of utility programs to aid the implementor, as well as training courses and manuals.

7.8 STATUS APPLICATIONS

It should be clear by now that a free text system, such as STATUS, can be used in a large number of application. Indeed it can be seen from the selection of users in Appendix I that STATUS is very widely used. In this section we will outline a few of these applications to show how a single text processing system can support a number of different user requirements.

7.8.1 Hazardous Chemicals Data Base

The aim of this system is to provide rapid identification of hazardous chemicals at the scene of an accident. The system, which is used by the fire brigade, must be simple to use and available 24 hours a day. Though all chemical containers should carry a HAZCHEM warning label, this may have been destroyed in the initial accident and so the chemical can only be identified by its container and its physical appearance; on the basis of this information the fire brigade have to decide what action to take.

Each article in the data base corresponds to one particular chemical. The article contains a description of the chemical, details of the types of container used to transport it and details of what action should be taken in the event of an emergency. The user interface has been kept as simple as possible and has been very carefully documented, from the details of switching on the terminal, through searching the data base, to logging off the system. The number of commands that have to be used has been kept to a minimum; for searching the data base only the question, sub-question and display commands need to be used. This application has shown that it is possible to design a text processing system that can be used by people with no previous computer experience.

7.8.2 European Law Centre

The aim of this system is to provide lawyers and others, with the full text of UK and EEC legislation and law reports. With the ever increasing volume of legal information it is becoming more and more difficult for individual lawyers to be familiar with, or even have ready access to, all the law relevant to their particular field.

The articles in the data base consist just of the text of individual statutes and case reports. No attempt is made to index these manually because of the large volume of text involved. But since legal text is precise and uses a well defined limited vocabulary, it is quite practical to search the original source text. The synonym and thesaurus facilities are very useful here for extending the scope of the search, and the browsing facility is very useful for looking at long legal documents. This system has shown that it is practical to store and search large volumes of free text without any manual classification.

7.8.3 North Sea Oil Production
The aim of this system is to provide monthly reports on the details of North Sea oil production. Individual oil companies provide information on the output of each well in various North Sea fields. From this data, the Department of Energy requires various reports giving details of the total production. The system must be sufficiently flexible to allow for changes to the format and content of the input data and also changes to the monthly reports.

Each article in the data base contains the production figures for a particular well. The individual figures have associated tags and these are used to identify the data when searching and producing reports. A great degree of flexibility is possible since there is no fixed format for the articles, and the proformas used for generating the reports can easily be changed. This application has shown that it is practical to use a text processing system for the storage and retrieval of numeric data.

7.8.4 Transport and Road Research Laboratory
The aim of this system is to provide an integrated library management facility for the TRRL Library. The system is used for library ordering, catalogue information and loan control. Each of these functions could be performed by an independent system but to reduce unnecessary duplication they have been combined into a single system.

Each article in the data base contains information about a particular book. As the book is processed through the library so the information in the article changes. Initially the article contains the author title and other information required to order the book. The system can then print out order list of books required from each bookseller. When the book arrives the article is updated to contain local catalogue information; this can either be searched on-line or used to produce a printed catalogue. Finally as books are lent to readers, and returned, the article is again updated; it is then possible to search the data base for books that are overdue and issue recall notices. Note that the macro facility can be used to reduce the effort involved in editing the articles. This system has shown that several different applications can be integrated into a single system.

7.9 SUMMARY

There is a naive view that to produce a computerised information system it is necessary only to type in the information and the machine will do the rest. Equally misleading is the view that all that is required is a 'good' retrieval algorithm. In this chapter we have attempted to show that any successful working system will require the integration of a number of complex computer procedures and manual procedures. Whilst it is possible to produce individual computer programs for each application, it is often more economical to use a tried and tested software package to perform the bulk of the computer processing. It should be noted that similar consideration apply to the development of the software package itself — it may be more economic to use existing software in the package rather than writing software specially for the package. Where there are benefits to the customer in using specially written software in the package, then this is often the overriding consideration.

We have described in some detail one particular information retrieval package, STATUS. The system is very large and we have not begun to describe its detailed workings. The main algorithms used in the system are quite simple, the bulk of the software is in the supporting procedures. However, as well as being simple the algorithms are also very general, and it is this that means the system can be used for such a wide range of applications.

The packages that are now available could be described as the first generation of text processing systems. The principal characterisation of such systems is that they deal with lexical and syntactic structures rather than with semantics, and that the algorithms they use to process these structures are strictly deterministic. There are, however, many research systems which overcome these limitations to a greater or lesser extent. We shall look at some of these methods in the final chapter, and try to form some views on the development of the next generation of information systems.

8

The Next Generation of Text Processing Systems

You progress not through improving what has been done, but reaching towards what has yet to be done.

Kahlil Gibran
Spiritual Sayings

8.1 THE IDEAL SYSTEM

To some people the ideal computerised information system is epitomised by HAL in the science fiction novel and film 2001 (Clarke 1968). HAL (heuristically programmed algorithmic computer) can understand human speech, can recognise events in his environment with television cameras and other sensors, has powerful deductive and problem solving capbilities and has a vast data base of readily accessible information. In fact it is quite possible to conduct an intelligent conversation with HAL. This idea of being able to conduct a conversation with a computer originated with the **Turing test** for machine intelligence. This test assumes that a subject is in a room with two computer terminals. The terminals are identical except that one is driven by a computer and the other by a human. The subject is asked to conduct a dialogue with each terminal to try and discover which is connected to the computer. If the subjects cannot distinguish between the computer and the human then the test says that the computer is, indeed, intelligent. Needless to say no machine has yet passed the Turing test, even if one did it could hardly be called the ideal system, since it performs no better than a human. The ideal system would need, in addition:

   (i) powerful deductive capabilities
   (ii) very large data base storage
   (iii) multi-lingual translation for input and output.
   etc. etc.

The development of such a system is even less likely and even if one did exist it would be unlikely to satisfy all of the people all of the time.

There is an important distinction between 'the ideal system' and 'a user's ideal system'. Throughout this book we have emphasized that the user's requirements are fundamental to the design of any text processing system. The concept of 'an ideal system' is misleading since it assumes that there is a universal description of the problems of information systems and that a solution to this can be found by an orderly scientific approach. This view is epitomised by calling the study of information systems a science — information science. It is worthwhile looking at a dictionary definition of science and then comparing it with the definition of engineering; the following definitions are taken from Chambers 20th Century Dictionary:

Science   — knowledge ascertained by observation and experiment, critically tested, systemised and brought under general principles

Engineering — the design, construction or use of engines or machines of any type.

The view of information systems that we have proposed is more closely related to engineering than to science, and we shall describe the subject as information engineering.

Once we have moved from a scientific to an engineering point of view, a number of changes are apparent. Principally, rather than asking the question 'What are the characteristics of the ideal system?' we should ask 'What are the objectives for this user's system?' In particular the following questions must be asked:

(i) What new information does the user want?
(ii) Why does he want this information?
(iii) What information does the user already have?

Only after these questions have been answered will it be possible to design a system to meet the user's requirements. And, when the system starts to produce results, rather than ask if these results are what one would expect from the ideal system, one should ask:

(iv) Are the results what the user wants?

This approach places many decisions on the user, and he may need some guidance on a suitable path to follow. There are a number of theoretical and practical limitations on what can be achieved; there are areas that have been well developed and areas that are still being developed and are not suitable for production systems. In the next few sections we will discuss these limitations in more detail, and conclude with a personal view of what may be achieved in the next generation of text processing systems.

8.2 THEORETICAL LIMITATIONS

In the previous section we argued that the user's objectives, rather than any idealised goals, should form the basis of any text processing system. This argument is further strengthened by the fact that there are a number of theoretical limitations to the capability of a general text processing system. To understand these limitations it is necessary to look at the logic and philosophy underlying the linguistic analysis, since this is what imposes the main theoretical limitations. We have seen in section 2.1 that linguistic analysis can be split into three areas:

    (i) lexical
   (ii) syntactic
  (iii) semantic.

The lexical analysis presents few problems. Indeed since the number of valid words is finite there is no theoretical limitations to performing a complete lexical analysis.

There are however limitations to the syntactic analysis. Consider the sentence:

    I met the old man who met the old man yesterday.

As it stands it is ambiguous, the adverb "yesterday" could be parsed either with the main verb or with the adjectival phrase. But this sentence can be extended by any number of repetitions of the phrase "who met the old man", and each addition introduces further ambiguities. Chomsky (1964) has shown that any attempt to use finite automaton to parse such sentences will eventually fail. (The automaton will not have enough space to remember all the parsings.) Thus on any finite machine, a complete syntactic analysis will be possible for only a finite number of the unbounded number of valid sentences.

The semantic analysis, the attempt to extract the meaning of a text, presents the most difficult problems. The underlying theory of meaning will place restrictions on the scope of the analysis. In the present context the most suitable theory to apply is logical positivism.

One of the classic statements of logical positivism is by A. J. Ayer (1936). He gives a criterion, the principle of verification, to test the significance of sentences. The principle states that a sentence is meaningful to a person if and only if he knows what observations would lead him to accept the sentence as true or reject it as false. Thus the sentence 'This is a book' should be meaningful to the reader, while 'Colourless green ideas sleep furiously.' is not. It could be argued that the latter expresses the proposition that the set of colourless green ideas is contained in the set of things that sleep furiously, and hence is a tautology since both sets are empty. Ayer says that tautologies have only an emotional significance, for example '(p.AND.q).IMPLIES.p' serves only to emphasise p in the conjunction of p and q, and so tautologies fall outside this theory. Therefore, we cannot expect the semantic analysis of a text processing system to deal with tautologies.

There are other sentences that fall outside the scope of the principle of verification, and so cannot be fully analysed. Consider the sentence 'All crows are black.' No finite number of observations could lead a logical person to accept this as true, though it could be rejected by a single observation. Thus it should be classified as meaningless, though it does convey some information. The confusion arises because the principle of verification is concerned with simple propositions, whilst the previous sentence involves the universal quantifier 'all'. Similar problems occur with sentences involving the ideas of truth and belief. (Is the sentence 'I believe all crows ar black.' meaningful?) Thus the principle of verification can be applied only to simple sentences which do not involve logical quantifiers or truth values, that is, statements from the primary language defined by Russell (1940). Though this argument applies only when the observable universe contains an unbounded number of elements, it seems reasonable to insist on the restriction to simple statements in all cases, since the more complex sentences require quite different methods.

Though this is the main restriction there are other cases where the principle fails. Consider the sentences

> Epimenides says "All Cretans are liars.".
>
> Epimenides is a Cretan.

Each sentence can be verified and so, according to the principle of verification, each sentence is meaningful, yet together they form a meaningless contradiction.

The paradox goes even deeper. Godel (1931) has shown how to number the symbols, formulae and proofs of a mathematical system, and using this numbering has produced a proposition, P, which states that P is not provable. This implies that there is a sentence, say S, which expresses the proposition 'There is a sentence that can not be verified and that sentence is S.' The S can be neither true nor false, since both lead to contradictions, yet the principle of verification says it is meaningful. Thus the theory, like mathematics, is incomplete; there are simple sentences it cannot handle. Note that the above sentence S corresponds to Epimenides' paradox; the first sentence states the existence of a class of false sentences and the second states that the first sentence is in this class. Epimenides has laid the basis of Godel's theory 2,500 years earlier.

So even before we begin to design a text processing system there are certain fundamental limitations that have to be accepted. Once we begin the design and implementation of the system then there is a whole range of practical limitations on what can be achieved.

8.3 PRACTICAL LIMITATIONS

There are three main factors that can impose practical limitations on the design and implementation of text processing systems. They are:

(i) size
(ii) time
(iii) cost.

We have already seen some of the limitations imposed by the size of the system — the more detailed types of data extraction that were described in section 4.5 and 4.6 can be applied to only a relatively small data bases. As a general principle, the size and diversity of the application area will limit the detail and depth of analysis that can be performed. This limitation is particularly severe in deductive systems where it is necessary to look at large numbers of combinations of data items before a useful deduction can be made. As the size of the data base grows so the number of possible combinations of data items increases very rapidly. This is known as a **combinatorial explosion**.

Size limitations also apply to other types of text processing systems. As a clustered file grows in size, so it takes increasingly longer to find a suitable cluster for any new text. What is worse, for some types of clustering algorithm (though not for the single link clustering algorithm of section 3.2.12) the addition of large numbers of new items can produce anomalous results. So it may be necessary to recluster the file periodically, and as the file grows this can become an increasingly costly operation. Similarly, as an indexed file grows in size it takes increasingly longer to index new text and it may be possible to overcome this only by a costly reorganisation of the index. But it is not only text input and analysis that are affected; the amount of work involved in data maintenance will also increase with the size of the data base. Indeed, for larger data bases the data validation and data integrity procedures have to be correspondingly stricter, to keep the number of errors to a minimum. It is important to realise that in most information systems 'more' does not necessarily mean 'better'. There will usually be an optimum size of data base and it is important to try to discover what it is.

As with many computer algorithms, some aspects of text processing systems show a trade-off between time and size. If the user requires a larger data base, then the time required to perform certain actions increases. Thus if there is a demand for a short response time then this can impose a restriction on the size of the data base. The acceptable response time will also place limits on the number of people who can use the system at any one time. In general, having a large number of users reading from a data base presents no real problems; the response time will be limited by the hardware and the operating system. It is more important to try to limit the number of people who are writing to the data base. As we saw at the end of section 7.3, each user must finish his own modification before another user can start to change related data; as the number of users increase, any one user may have to wait an unacceptably long time to perform his particular modification. So maintaining a reasonable response time may involve limiting the number of users who can modify the data base; in the extreme case, all modifications can be directed to the data base manager for a batch update.

Many of the practical limitations we have discussed are, in the end, limitations on cost. Building and maintaining a large data base is an expensive business, both in manual effort and in computer resources. So the amount of money that the user is prepared to spend will significantly affect the type of system that he is given. Ultimately the user will have to decide if the performance of the system justifies its cost.

8.4 ASSESSING PERFORMANCE

It is important to have an effective method of assessing the performance of a text processing system. This can be used not only to help measure the cost effectiveness of existing systems, but also to test new methods of text processing for use in the next generation of systems. The measurement of performance, however, is one of the more difficult and less well studied areas of text processing. A number of tools are available, which can be grouped under the following headings:

    (i) user surveys
    (ii) relevance measures
    (iii) modelling.

The principle behind user surveys is quite simple: since the aim of any text processing system is to meet the requirements of a group of users, then the best way to assess the performance of the system is to ask its users. As with any other type of survey, the nature of questions that are asked can significantly affect the final result of the survey. If this type of technique is to be successful, then the survey should cover not only the results the user has obtained from the system, but also how easily he obtained those results, what the use of the system cost him, and if the reults justified the cost and effort involved. A sample of the type of questionnaire that could be used is given in Fig. 8.1.

Please circle the reply that best answers each question.

(1) Did you find the system easier or harder to use than you expected?
    (a) much easier   (b) easier   (c) much as I expected
    (d) harder   (e) much harder

(2) Have you used this system or a similar system before?
    (a) Yes   (b) No

(3) Have you used a computer terminal before?
    (a) Yes   (b) No

(4) How many useful documents did the system produce?
    (a) None   (b) 1-4   (c) 5-10   (d) 10-20
    (e) over 20

(5) How much would you be prepared to pay for using the system?
    (a) nothing   (b) 25p   (c) 50p   (d) 75p
    (e) over £1

Fig. 8.1 –Sample questionnaire from a user survey.

While user surveys attempt to assess the overall performance of a system, relevance measures attempt to make a more accurate measurement of one particular area of text processing systems, namely document retrieval. A question presented to a document retrieval system should elicit a list of documents relevant to the original question. If the data base is relatively small then it may be possible to search through it all and identify those documents that are considered relevant. This manually prepared list can then be compared with the system response. Before we look at any of the measures that are used to compare responses it should be emphasised that these measures all rely on an 'expert' opinion of what documents are relevant to a given question. Each user will have his own concept of what is or is not relevant to his information need; these concepts of relevance may be in agreement with the 'expert' but they may differ significantly.

For systems which do not produce ranked output, most relevance measures are based on the contingency table shown in Fig. 8.2. This represents the result of a single search, through a data base of N documents, to retrieve documents relevant to a single user question. The system has retrieved $(a+b)$ documents and of these a are relevant to the user and b are not relevant; similarly of the $(c+d)$ documents that have not been retrieved, c would have been relevant and d are not relevant. This leads to a concept of an ideal system where b and c are zero. There are a number of ways of measuring how well a particular system matches up to this ideal; the most widely used are recall and precision.

	Relevant	Not Relevant
Retrieved	a	b
Not Retrieved	c	d

$a + b + c + d = N$ (number of documents)

Fig. 8.2 – Relevance contingency table.

8.4.1 Definition
The recall, R, of a system in response to a question is the ratio of the number of relevant documents that have been retrieved to the total number of relevant documents, that is,

$$R = a/(a + c)$$

The precision P, is the ratio of the number of relevant documents that have been retrieved to the total number of retrieved documents, that is

$$P = a/(a + b)$$

Note that in an 'ideal' system $P = R = 1$, but in practice P and R are usually less than 1. □

8.4.2 Example

Consider the two contingency tables shown in Fig. 8.3. In both cases $R = P = 0.9$, but the behaviour of the system in each case is quite different. In table (i) the user has received a good response to what was probably a fairly specific question, while in table (ii) the user has received very little new information — he still has over 800 documents to look at. □

	Relevant	Not Relevant
Retrieved	9	1
Not Retrieved	1	989

(i)

	Relevant	Not Relevant
Retrieved	810	90
Not Retrieved	90	10

(ii)

Fig. 8.3 – Limitation of recall and precision.

Recall and precision can also be used to measure the performance of ranked output systems. In this case pairs of recall and precision values are calculated from the first n documents in the ranked output, for $n = 1, 2, 3 \ldots$ These values can then be plotted on an R–P graph as shown in Fig. 8.4. It should be noticed that in this type of graph, recall and precision are always inversely related; in general the higher the recall the lower the precision. It is possible to average these graphs over a number of different searches and so obtain some measure of

Ranked Output	Relevant
1	✓
2	✓
3	x
4	x
5	✓
6	x
7	x
8	✓
9	x
10	x

No. Retrieved $(a+b)$	No. Relevant (a)	R	P
1	1	0.2	1.0
2	2	0.4	1.0
3	2	0.4	0.66
4	2	0.4	0.5
5	3	0.6	0.6
6	3	0.6	0.5
7	3	0.6	0.47
8	4	0.8	0.5
9	4	0.8	0.44
10	4	0.8	0.4

Note the recall values assume a total of 5 relevant documents in the data base.

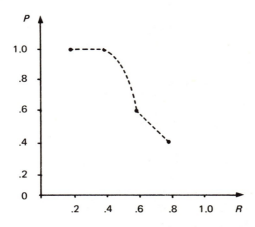

Note for any given R value it is customary to plot only the largest corresponding P value.

Fig. 8.4 – R-P curve for ranked output.

the performance of the system as a whole. These results, however, are very much affected by the type of data base, questions and relevance judgements that are used, and it is very difficult to make sensible comparisons between different systems. One factor that did emerge from a recent study by McGill (1979) was that no existing ranking algorithm (as in the definition of section 4.3.1) produces an improvement of more than 20%. The conclusion was that the existing methods are not using all the variables necessary to produce an effective system. More information on methods of measuring retrieval performance can be found in Van Rijsenberg (1975).

A final method of assessing performance is to build a model of the system. It should be possible to build a model which can be used to predict the optimum performance of the system. The actual performance can then be compared with this optimum performance and a measure of the efficiency obtained. This can be used to study various strategies in a standard retrieval environment; it is, however, more useful in complex text processing. Consider again the pharmaceutical system of section 6.2.2; it is naturally important that there should be high precision and recall on the identification of drugs, but these values on their own do not provide an adequate assessment of the performance of the whole system. To do this it would be necessary to model the use of the system, number of enquiries, cost of each enquiry etc.

The main yardstick for measuring the performance of experimental systems has been the R–P graph. We have seen that this has a number of limitations and if the next generation of text processing systems is to advance significantly then some new method of assessing performance will be required.

8.5 THE COMMERCIAL ENVIRONMENT

We have emphasised throughout this chapter that the design of the next generation of text processing systems should be determined by the users' requirements. These requirements, however, will depend on the environment, and in particular the commercial environment, of the user. So to get some idea of what will be required of future systems, it is necessary to look at the present commercial environment, not just of the user, but also of the software supplier and the data base supplier.

The installation of a text processing system in a commercial environment is often a very difficult task. The initial decision to automate is often taken for confused and sometimes even wrong reasons (Wessel 1980). The goals that management set are frequently changing and in many cases impracticable. The reason for such a state of affairs is that the manager responsible for the project often has little appreciation of what is and is not practical. So if things are to improve with the next generation of systems then, in the commercial environment, there must be a greater understanding of what such systems can do. At present there seems to be a large gap in the information field between the systems that have been developed in the computer laboratories and the systems that have been implemented in the commercial world. This gap should be bridged by the engineering approach that was advanced at the beginning of this chapter.

The on-line bibliographic retrieval systems operate in a rather different environment. The original ideal of an on-line terminal on every scientist's desk or engineer's bench has not been fulfilled, instead most searching is performed by library intermediaries using only a small number of the facilities available. In general the searchers do not appear to be interested in new features such as ranking or feed-back but are more concerned about stability and maintenance of the existing system and minor cosmetic changes.

The major data base suppliers tend to be publishers involved in producing printed indexes and other reference works. This has a number of implications for the on-line data bases; in particular as regards standardisation and duplication. Since the data base suppliers' main business is usually publishing reference works, there is little incentive to try to standardise the on-line data. At the same time they do not want to remove references that are duplicated in other data bases, since this would reduce their royalty. These factors have led to the situation where in some areas there may be up to 50% duplication of references and a single reference may even be entered and indexed on seven different files. It seems unlikely that this state of affairs will change within the next five years.

Once a text processing system has been established, it is very difficult to change it. The users will have become accustomed to the existing system and the introduction of a new system will involve time and effort in changing operating procedures. In addition, the software suppliers may be unwilling to embark on costly new development. The next generation of text processing systems is likely to appear in areas where there are no existing computerised systems. Indeed this effect has already been seen with full text searching – this was first introduced into legal data base systems, where there was little previous computerisation, rather than into existing bibliographic systems.

8.6 CURRENT RESEARCH

In the main body of this book we have discussed various aspects of text processing. In this section we will look at some of the research that is currently being undertaken in these areas; it is convenient to group it under three headings:

    (i) optimisation
    (ii) enhancement
    (iii) innovation.

As systems grow, both in terms of data base size and number of users, it becomes increasingly important that they should operate efficiently. There is considerable effort being devoted to optimising the performance of existing types of system. In this area we have already discussed the development of text compression (section 3.3) and content addressable memories (section 3.5). As well as this, there is a lot of work being done on the storage of the analysed text. For clustered files, this involves improved clustering algorithms; some examples of these can be found in Salton and Wong (1978). Compression techniques can also be applied to the reference file in a Boolean system; the reference lists can be anything from a few items to several thousand items long. The long reference lists can, in some cases, be more efficiently stored as run length coded binary vectors. The reference list for a word is regarded as a binary vector where a 1 or 0 in the ith position indicates the presence or absence of the word in the ith document. This vector can then be stored in a run-length coded form as in section 3.7. For more details of this approach see Schuegraf (1976). Finally, efficient implementation of large relational data bases has proved very difficult. Only recently has it seemed possible to support a large multi-user relational system; an overview of an experimental system is given by Blasgen *et al.* (1981).

At the present time most data base systems are operating on conventional hardware. We have, however, already mentioned the use of content addressable memories and there are other types of special purpose hardware that can be used to improve the performance of existing types of system. With Boolean systems, the main area of research is in the use of 'back-end' processors to evaluate the Boolean search functions. This can involve the merging of many long reference lists and some form of parallel processor is ideally suited to the task; a description of one type of hardware that has been used is given by Stellhorn (1977). Parallel and vector processors are well suited to computing the similarity co-efficients used in ranking and clustering methods. If this hardware produces significant improvements then those methods may become commercially viable. The use of computer networks and distributed computing could have a significant effect on all types of information systems. The principle of a distributed data base is to concatinate a number of small local data bases into a single logical data base. This means that many of the data base management functions can be performed locally on a fairly small scale, and that if any required data is not available locally, then all the other data bases can be searched automatically.

Since it is clear that the present generation of text processing systems are going to continue in use for some considerable time, there is a lot of research into methods of enhancing the existing systems. These enhancements can be split into two classes, those that are independent of the host system and those that are integrated with it. As we have seen, there is little possibility of any major changes to the on-line bibliographic systems and so some users have set about developing their own independent enhancements. The standard method is to use an intelligent, rather than a dumb, terminal to connect the user with the host system. One such device has been developed by Williams (1980). Another, more ambitious, system is being developed at the National Library of

Medicine (Horowitz *et al.* 1979). The system employs an intelligent terminal to generate commands to, and capture output from on-line data base systems. The terminal can, to a limited extent, transform data output by one system into input to another system and substitute data files for keyboard input. At present the system uses the NLM, Lockheed, CIS, RECON and NIOSHTIC on-line systems. The transformation programs can take selected text from some of these files and convert it into search statements for use on another. For example a search on CHEMLINE could give a list of chemical registry numbers, this output can then be converted to a series of commands to search CA CONDENSATES for these registry numbers. A similar system is being developed by Marcus and Reintjes (1979). One problem with such systems is the tendency to regard the host system as a batch processor and so loose the benefits of the user interacting with the system. This problem may be less severe if the enhancements are integrated into the main system.

The commercial software packages and experimental systems have much more scope for making enhancements. We have already seen (section 7.5) how a number of advanced features have been integrated into the STATUS system. Ranked output and feedback is already in use in many research systems, though as yet they have made little impact on the commercial packages. There is much study into the best types of indexing and ranking; the study by McGill (1979) lists 39 different weighting functions and 67 different similarity coefficients. Lastly, there is a growing interest in the problems of multi data base searching. As the number of data bases grows then it becomes increasingly difficult to select a suitable data base for a given search. Williams (1979) has studied possible methods of data base selection; an alternative approach is to concatinate a number of data bases and then search them simultaneously, though this too has its problems (Hawkins 1978).

The third heading, innovative research, covers a very wide field. A number of people are studying the underlying assumptions of information retrieval in an attempt to aid the development of improved systems. One such area of research is based on the notion that the decision to assign a given index term to a document should be based on expected utility of that decision for all potential users. This utility, theoretic indexing, has been described by Cooper and Maron (1978). In common with other manual indexing methods, this approach can lead to problems of 'output overload'. This occurs if most documents have been assigned only two or three index terms, then any attempt to increase the precision of a search by coordinating more index terms will make it very likely that no documents will be retrieved at all. Some of the present research is directed to overcoming this problem by applying the utility-theoretic indexing to provide ranked output. The proposed ranking method should be able to take account of such factors as language and journal of publication. Belkin (1980) is looking at a similar problem by formalising the user's need for information and taking this as a basis for indexing and searching the data base.

Other research workers have moved out of the field of document retrieval to more 'intelligent' text processing systems. The first important system of this kind was probably that developed by Winograd (1972). Since then a large number of such systems have been described in the literature, one of the more recent is that developed by Schank *et al.* (1981). This system analyses press reports about the US Secretary of State and uses them to build up a data base which can be interrogated by natural language questions. In this section we should also include systems where the source text is analysed manually before being stored for subsequent use. One such system is LEGOL (Stamper 1976); here the text of Acts of Parliament are manually analysed into a formal language, these legal formulae can then be used to manipulate data relating to a particular case and arrive at a judgement for that case.

Finally, an area of research that is becoming increasingly important is personal data bases. As the cost of computing falls it becomes possible for more people to keep their own data either on a bureau machine or on their own mini-computer. This poses a number of problems in the user interface, security and data transfer; research is just beginning into these problems.

8.7 HYBRID SYSTEMS

Throughout this book we have assumed, implicitly, that in a computerised text processing system all the text is stored in the computer and that the analysed text will provide the user with all the information he requires. In his recent book, Wessel (1980) has given examples of cases where total computerisation has proved too complex to work satisfactorily. In these situation there is a need for hybrid systems where the computer can act as a tool to perform specified tasks and the user supplies the intellectual effort required to complete the task.

This type of hybrid system is well illustrated by the work on computer aided indexing at the National Library of Medicine. This work makes use of the Associative Interactive Dictionary (AID) and the Current Information Transfer in English (CITE) systems. But these systems are based on the TOXLINE and MEDLINE data bases at NLM. The CITE system will take an English language sentence, identify the keywords and process them. This processing involves extracting the postings list from the data base, merging these lists and then ranking the documents. The documents can then be output and the free text terms and index terms of the relevant documents are used to modify the search. Given that the user has retrieved a set of relevant documents the AID system can be used to identify conceptual text associations. This is based on the assumption that if a term occurs more frequently in the retrieved set than in the rest of the collection, then that term is semantically related to the original information request. One of the applications of this is as an aid to indexing; article abstracts can be entered into CITE to retrieve similar documents and AID can then be used to identify the associated index terms. Both these systems are described in more detail by Doszkocs (1978) and Doszkocs and Rapp (1979).

Though the cost of computer storage is decreasing it is not always economic to keep large volumes of text in computer stores. This gives rise to yet another type of hybrid system, where the main body of text is kept on some computer controlled storage device with only the index in computer storage. The most common type of device is the computer controlled micro-fiche; though computer controlled video-discs, which can store up to 20,000 pages of text on a single 10″ disc, are likely to become increasingly important. These devices are efficient for storing fixed text but they are read-only and so updating the text involves making a new disc. One alternative is to use video-tapes; these have a similar capacity to video-discs, are much easier to update but have an appreciably longer access time. In all cases the text is stored in optical form and must be transmitted to the user in this form. The alternatives are either to have a copy of the data at each remote user site and present the optical image directly to the user, or else have a single central store and some means of facsimile transmission to each remote user site.

Though the use of on-line terminals for searching is increasing, there is still a demand for printed indexes. This type of hybrid system — manual searching of computer produced indexes — has a number of advantages:

   (i) low cost — no 'connect time' charges for on-line computer use

  (ii) availability — the printed index is always available for searching, whilst the computer system or communications network may be out of action for some part of the day

 (iii) familiarity — many users feel more at home with a printed index than with a computer terminal.

Because of these advantages, such hybrid systems should not be rejected just because they appear out of date. The advent of computer output micro-fiche (COM) means that it is now possible to produce and distribute large indexes cheaply and quickly. In addition the use of key word in context (KWIC) has meant that printed indexes can be used much more efficiently. (For each key-word, a KWIC index gives not only a list of documents indexed by that word but also each line of the text in which that word occurs; this gives the user some indication as to whether or not the document will be relevant).

It is important to realise that, with the present state of knowledge, total computerisation will not be the answer to every user's requirements. The aim of a text processing system should be to satisfy the user not the system programmer; in some cases this can best be achieved by the use of hybrid systems such as we have described in this section.

8.8 MULTIPLE SYSTEMS

As the use of text processors increases it will become less and less efficient to store all the text in a single central location. There are a number of reasons for this:

(i)   data transfer − if one part of the data base is searched and maintained mainly by a group of users at a particular location, then it is more efficient to store and maintain the data locally rather than have to keep transferring it to and from the central store.

(ii) contention − if a number of people want to modify information in the data base and that information is all stored on the same physical device, then each user will have to wait his turn to modify the data base − this could cause serious delays for the user at the end of the queue.

(iii) data format − the text in the central store may not be in a format that is suitable for processing at a remote user's site.

Because of these problems there is a tendency towards individual systems at each user's site rather than a single central system. This has a number of consequences not least on system integration. If these multiple systems are to co-operate successfully then there are several areas that need careful consideration:

(i)   network facilities − if the systems are to co-operate then they must be able to communicate, this requires an efficient network facility to enable users at each site to access a system at any other site.

(ii) data portability − wherever possible there should be a standard format for the interchange of information so text output from one system can be directly input to another system

(iii) file conversion − where standard interchange formats have not been agreed then there should be efficient utilities to convert the output format of one system into the input format of another

(iv) common commands − each system should support a set of standard common commands to perform the basic information retrieval functions, (in addition to the commands peculiar to each particular system).

These problems have received various amounts of study. It is now possible for users and computers at remote sites to communicate but it is by no means as simple and efficient as it might be. Some effort has been devoted to data portability; in particular the MARC format is now widely used for transfer of bibliographic information. File conversion is still a difficult problem and is usually tackled on a 'one-off' basis. Some work has been done on defining a common command language (Negus 1977) but as yet few systems have adopted this language.

8.9 THE NEXT GENERATION OF IR SYSTEMS

There are at present several different types of information retrieval systems. These can be grouped under three main headings:

(a)   Document retrieval

   (b) DBMS
   (c) Question answering.

There have been some attempts at combining these into a single system and it seems likely that there will be a significant move towards such integrated systems. This is likely to become more important with the growth of non-textual information systems.

Another important distinction is that between public and private information systems. There is already a growing amount of research in developing personal information systems and in tailoring the public systems for special applications. With a sufficiently flexible user interface and suitable security checks it should be possible to build these options into the next generation of text processing systems.

As well as considering the functions provided by information systems it is also important to consider the method of implementation. In the next generation of systems it will probably be possible to implement some parts of them on special purpose architectures. This will require, however, that the system be designed as a series of modules which can be implemented in hardware or software as appropriate.

Finally it is important to realise that there will not be just one new system but a whole range of systems. The power and use of these systems will be greatly enhanced if there is a simple, standard method of transferring information from one system to another; just because data is in machine readable form does not mean it is instantly available to any information system.

This review of some of the current research on information retrieval seems to suggest that the next generation of IR systems should provide a comprehensive and compatible set of tools for processing all types of information. To develop such a system more work needs to be done in the following areas:

   (i) User interface; to develop interfaces free from the limitations of command languages and menu systems.
   (ii) Data base interfaces; to develop distributed data bases so that it is easy to move information from one system to another, in particular between document retrieval, DBMS and question answering systems.
   (iii) System interfaces; to develop modular systems to take full use of distributed networks and special purpose architecture.

It is important to remember, however, that any text processing system will be used in live applications and so it must always match the requirements and capabilities of the end user.

Bibliography

Adamson, G. W. and Boreham, J. (1974), The use of an associative measure based on character structure to identify semantically related words and document titles, *Information Processing and Management*, **10**, No. 7, pp. 253-260.

Aho, A. V. and Ullman, J. D. (1973), *The Theory of parsing, translating and compiling*. Prentice-Hall.

Anderson, G. A. and Kain, R. Y. (1976). A content addressed memory designed for data base applications. Proceedings of the 1976 International Conference on Parallel Processing, *IEEE*.

Anderson, M. L. B. (1976). *Cybernetics and Acts of Parliament*, 3rd Annual Conference of the Cybernetics Society, London.

Anderson, M. L. B. (1977). *Capturing legal data using optical recognition techniques*. Social Science Research Council, London.

Ashford, J. H. (1980). Information management packages on mini-computers. *Journal of Information Science*, **2**, pp. 23-28.

Ashford, J. H. and Matkin, D. I. (1980). Report on a study of the potential users and application areas for free text information storage and retrieval systems in Britain. *Program* **14**, No. 1, pp. 14-23.

Ayer, A. J. (1936). *Language, Truth and Logic*. Reprinted by Penguin.

Backus, J. W. (1960). The syntax and semantics of the proposed international algebraic language of the Zurich ACM-GAMM conference. *Proceedings of the 1959 International Conference on Information Processing*, pp. 125-132, Butterworths.

Belkin, N. J. (1980). Anomalous state of knowledge as a basis for information retrieval. *Canadian Journal of Information Science*, **5**, pp. 132-143.

Blasgen, M. W., Astrahan, M. M., Chamberlin, D. D., Gray, J. N., King, W. F., Lindsey, B. G., Lorie, R. A., Mehl, J. W., Price, T. G., Pouzolu, G. R., Schkolnick, M., Selinger, P. G., Slutz, D. R., Strong, H. R., Traiger, I. L., Wade, B. W. and Yost, R. A. (1981). System R: An architectural overview. *IBM System Journal*, **20**, No. 1, pp. 41-61.

Bing, J. and Harvold, T. (1977). *Legal Decisions and Information Systems.* Global (for Universitetsforlaget).

Bobrow, D. G., Kaplan, R. M., Kay, M., Norman, D. A., Thompson, H. and Winograd, T. (1977). GUS, a frame driven dialog system. *Artificial Intelligence,* **8**, pp. 155-173.

Bolt, R. A. (1979). *Spatial Data Management.* Massachusetts Institute of Technology.

Boreham, J. and Niblett, G. B. F. (1976). Classification of legal texts by Computer, *Information Processing and Management,* **12**, pp. 125-132.

Brown, P. J. (1974). *Macro Processors.* John Wiley, London.

Chomsky, N. (1964). *Syntactic Structures.* Mouton, The Hague.

Clarke, A. C. (1968). *2001, A Space Odyssey.* Hutchinson, London.

Codd, E. F. (1970). A relational model of data for large shared data banks. *Communications of the ACM,* **13**, pp. 377-387.

Codd, E. F. (1971). A data base sublanguage founded on the relational calculus. *Proceedings of the 1971 ACM SIGFIDET Workshop on data description, access and control.*

Coleman, C. F. (1976). *A word and digraph frequency analysis of five legal texts.* (AERE R85 07) HMSO, London.

Cooper, W. S. and Maron, M. E. (1978). Foundations of probabilistic and utility theoretic indexing. *Journal of the ACM,* **25**, No. 1, pp. 67-80.

Date, C. J. (1975). *An introduction to database systems.* Addison Wesley, London.

Doszkocs, T. E. (1978). An associative interactive dictionary (AID) for on-line bibliographic searching. *Proceedings of the ASIS 41st Annual Meeting,* **15**, pp. 105-109.

Doszkocs, T. E. and Rapp, B. A. (1979). Searching MEDLINE in English: A prototype user interface with natural language query, ranked output and relevance feedback. *Proceedings of the ASIS 42nd Annual Meeting,* **16**, pp. 131-139.

Earl, L. L. (1972). The resolution of syntactic ambiguity in automated language processing. *Information Storage and Retrieval,* **8**, pp. 277-308.

Freeman, F. H. (1976). Building a thesaurus for a diffuse subject area. *Special Libraries,* **67**, No. 4, pp. 220-222.

Godel, K. (1931). *On formally undecidable propositions of Principa Mathematica.* (English translation Oliver and Boyd, Edinburgh 1962).

Goldstein, C. M. and Ford, W. H. (1978). The user cordial interface. *On-line Review,* **2**, No. 3, pp. 269-275.

Goldstein, I. P. and Bobrow, D. G. (1980). Extending object oriented programming in smalltalk. *Proceedings of the 1980 Lisp Conference,* Palo Alto.

Hawkins, D. T. (1978). Multiple database searching techniques and pitfalls. *On-line,* **2**, No. 2, pp. 9-15.

Horowitz, A. J., Low, D. A. and Eastlake, D. E. (1979). *Design of a system for pre-prototype use of the Chemical Substances Information Network.* (CCA-79-26) Computer Corporation of America, Massachusetts.

Hsiao, D. K. and Baum, R. I. (1976). Information secure systems. *Advances in Computers,* **14**, pp. 231-271.

Ingemarsson, I. and Wong, G. K. (1981). A user authentication scheme for shared data based on a trap-door one-way function. *Information Processing Letters,* **12**, No. 2, pp. 63-67.

Irvine, R. (1972). *MARC for cataloguers.* University of Southampton.

Jardine, N. and Sibson, R. (1971). *Mathematical Taxonomy.* John Wiley, London.

Knuth, D. E. (1973). The art of Computer Programming Vol. 3. Sorting and Searching. Addison Wesley, Reading, Mass.

Lea W. A. (1980). Speech recognition: Past, present and future. (in *Trends in Speech Recognition,* (editor) W. A. Lea, Prentice-Hall, New Jersey).

Lee, R. M. (1977). Micro APP – a building block for low cost, high speed associative parallel processing. *The Radio and Electronic Engineer,* **47**, No. 3, pp. 91-99.

Luhn, H. P. (1957). A statistical approach to mechanised encoding and searching of library information. *IBM Journal of Research and Development,* **1**, pp. 309-317.

Maggs, P. B. (1974). Compression of legal texts for more economical computer storage. *Jurimetrics Journal,* **14**, pp. 254-261.

Marcus, R. S. and Reintjes, J. F. (1979). *Experiments and analysis on a computer interface to an information retrieval network.* (LIDS-R-900) Massachusetts Institute of Technology.

McGill, M. (1979). *An evaluation of factors affecting document ranking by information retrieval systems.* (NSF-IST-78-10454) Syracuse University, New York.

Negus, A. E. (1977). *EURONET guideline: Standard commands for retrieval systems.* Commission of European Community.

Olle, T. W. (1978). *The CODASYL approach to database management.* John Wiley, Chichester.

Robinson, A. J. (1965). A machine oriented logic based on the resolution principle. *Journal of the ACM,* **12**, No. 1, pp. 23-41.

Russell, B. (1940). *An enquiry into meaning and truth.* (Reprinted by Penguin, London).

Salton, G. (1968). *Automatic information organisation and retrieval.* McGraw-Hill, New York.

Salton, G. (1975). *Theory of Indexing.* Society of Industrial and Applied Mathematics.

Salton, G. and Wong, A. (1978). Generation and search of clustered files. *ACM Transactions on Database Systems,* **3**, No. 4, pp. 321-346.

Schank, R. C., Kolodner, J. L. and De Jong, G. (1981). Conceptual information retrieval (in *Information Retrieval Research,* (editor) R. N. Oddy, Butterworths).

Schuegraf, E. J. (1976). Compression of large inverted files with hyperbolic term distribution. *Information Processing and Management,* **12**, pp. 377-384.

Severance, D. and Duhne, R. (1976). A practitioner's guide to addressing algorithms. *Communications of the ACM,* **19**, No. 6, pp. 314-326.

Shannon, C. E. (1949). Communication in the presence of noise. *Proceedings of the Institute of Radio Engineers,* **37**, pp. 10-21.

Sibley, E. H. (1976). The development of database technology. *Computing Surveys,* **8**, pp. 1-7.

Spark Jones, K. and Kay, M. (1973). *Linguistics and information science,* Academic Press, New York.

Stamper, R. K. (1976). *The LEGOL project: a survey.* (SC 0081) IBM UK.

Stellhorn, W. H. (1977). An inverted file processor for information retrieval. *IEEE Transactions in Computing,* **C26**, No. 12, pp. 1258-1267.

Teskey, F. N. (1978). *A new method of processing textual material by cybernetic machine.* Ph.D. Thesis, University of London.

Teskey, F. N. (1980). STATUS and integrated information systems. *Journal of Documentation,* **36**, No. 1, pp. 33-41.

Thurber, K. J. and Wald, L. D. (1975). Associative and parallel processing. *Computing Surveys,* **7**, pp. 215-255.

Todd, S. J. P. (1976). The Peterlee relational test vehicle – a system overview. *IBM System Journal,* **15**, No. 4, pp. 285-308.

Turn, R. (1977). Privacy protection in information systems. *Advances in Computers,* **16**, pp. 221-336.

Van Rijsenberg, C. J. (1975). *Information Retrieval.* Butterworths, London.

Verhofstad, J. S. M. (1978). Recovery techniques for data base systems. *Computing Surveys,* **10**, pp. 168-195.

Wessel, A. E. (1980). *The implementation of complex information systems.* John Wiley, New York.

Wilks, Y. (1975). An intelligent analyser and understander of English. *Communications of the ACM,* **18**, pp. 264-274.

Williams, M. E. (1979). *Automatic data base selection and overlap of terms among major databases.* 7th Cranfield Conference, IEE.

Williams, P. W. (1980). Intelligent access to on-line systems. *Proceedings of the 4th International On-Line Information meeting,* On-line, London.

Wilson, C. W. J., Haynes, E. M. and Teskey, F. N. (1981). Harwell automated loans system – HAL, using STATUS. *Program,* **15**, No. 2, pp. 43-65.

Winograd, T. (1972). *Understanding natural language.* Academic Press, New York.

Woods, W. A., Kaplan, R. M. and Nash-Webber, B. (1972). *The lunar sciences natural language system*. Bolt, Beranek and Newman, Cambridge, Mass.

Yu, C. T., Luk, W. S. and Cheung, T. Y. (1976). A statistical model for relevance feedback in information retrieval. *Journal of the ACM*, **23**, pp. 273–286.

Zadeh, I. A. (1965). Fuzzy Sets. *Information and Control*, **8**, pp. 338–353.

List of Algorithms

Appendices I–IV

APPENDIX I — INFORMATION RETRIEVAL PACKAGES

There are now a very large number of information retrieval packages. Some of these have been developed and are used for just one particular application, others are actively marked and used in a wide range of applications. Rather than try to provide a comprehensive and up-to-date list of all packages we have listed just some of the systems that are available. A more comprehensive list of packages can be found in the current issue of *Computer Users Year Book, Directory of Software.*

Name	*Supplier*	*Comments*
ADABAS	Adabas Software Ltd Laurie House 22 Colyear Street Derby DE1 1CA.	Comprehensive and widely used DBMS system with capabilities for free text.
ADLIB } ADMIN }	L.M.R. Ltd 54 Moorbridge Road Maidenhead Berks SL6 8BN.	Wide range of library and information features.
ASSASSIN	Agricultural Division I.C.I. Ltd Billingham Cleveland TS23 1LB.	Well established in SDI and KWOC index, with new on-line search version.
BASIS	Batell Institute 505 King Avenue Columbas Ohio 43201.	Large, comprehensive free text system
CAIRS	Leatherhead Food R.A. Randal Road Leatherhead Surrey.	Mini-computer system oriented to controlled language bibliographic files.

DATABOSS	Turnkey Software Ltd 12 High Street Chalfont St. Giles Bucks HP8 4QA.	DBMS system with an extension for mixed text and data files.
DECO	Unilever Computer Services Station House Harrow Road Wembley HA9 6EB.	Simple user-friendly free text system.
DOCUMASTER	T.S.I. International 19 Bedford Row London WC1R 4EB	Full text system with efficient text indexing.
FACTFINDER	Mini-computer Systems Park House Park Street Maidenhead Berks	Integrated word processing, text retrieval and report generation.
INQUIRE	Infodata Systems Ltd 5205 Leesburg Pike Falls Church Virginia	Comprehensive and widely used IR package.
ORBIT	System Development Corp 2500 Colorado Avenue Santa Monica California 90406	Large, comprehensive free text system
SCRAPBOOK	Triad Computing Systems 42 Kingsway London WC2	Flexible free text system.
STAIRS	IBM UK Ltd 384 Chiswick High Road London W4 4AC.	Comprehensive and well documented IR package
STATUS	Computer Science and Systems Division A.E.R.E. Harwell Oxon OX11 0RA.	Well established portable free text system.

Each of these packages is used in a wide variety of applications. A selection of some of the uses of just one of these packages (STATUS) is given next page.

STATUS: A selection of users and applications

Name	Applications	Status*	Approx. Records	Approx. data	Computer
Attorney-General's Department (Australia)	Legal Information System	o	40,000	80Mb	Burroughs B6700
	Departmental opinions	o	1,000	½Mb	
BNF Metals Technology Centre	BNF Abstracts and Retrieval	o	20,000	10Mb	Prime 300 (224 kb)
	Company information	o	1,000	½Mb	
BOC Ltd	Document management	o	2,500		IBM/Amdahl (8Mb)
	Technical Abstracts (properties of gases)	o	500	1/10Mb	
Building Research Establishment (DoE)	Library database (Books and periodicals)	o	40,000	16Mb	Prime 300 (256 kb)
	Research project data for management	o	500		
	Reports of building faults	d	6,000	12Mb	
	Inventory of instruments	p	2,000		
Commission of the European Community	CELEX (Community Law)	d	30,000	120Mb	ICL 2980 (7Mb)
	Internals Documentation ECO_1	d	110,000	300Mb	
	Actualities	d	20,000	12Mb	
	Proposals to Council of Ministers	d	4,500	12Mb	
Department of Energy	North Sea Oil Production System	o	400	10Mb	IBM 3033 (8Mb)
Department of Health (Australia)	National drug information service	o	100	2Mb	IBM 370
European Law Centre (EUROLEX)	UK and EEC legislation, cases etc.	d	100,000	200Mb	IBM/Amdahl (8Mb)
Home Office	Hazardous Chemicals Database	o	10,000	15Mb	IBM/Amdahl
Howson-Algraphy Group, Vickers Ltd	Technical Abstracts	o	5,000	3Mb	ICL 2904 (96 kw)
	Index of internal reports	o	700		
	Product formulae (Health and Safety)	d	150		

Organisation	Application	Status*	No. of records	Storage	Computer
	Legal literature	o		10Mb	(2 × 256 kw)
	Legislation	d		20Mb	
Metal Box Ltd	Technical Reports	o/d	2,000	6Mb	ICL 1904 (32 kw)
	Library Catalogue entries	o/d	3,000	5Mb	
	Literary Loan records	d			
Ricardo Consulting Engineers Ltd	Technical Abstracts	d			ICL 2904 (96 kw)
	Engine database	d			
Rutherford Laboratory (SRC)	Internals manuals	o	300		Prime 400 (1Mb)
	Personal literature database	o	100		
	Engineering drawing specifications	d	11,000		
	Equipment Holdings	d	330		
Safety in Mines Research Establishment (H and SE)	Library Catalogue	o	10,000	10Mb	XEROX Sigma 6 (128k)
	Chemical Substances Database	o	12,000	12Mb	
	Accident Studies	d	1,200		
	Toxic chemicals data	p	50,000		
	Factory Inspector's Report	p			
Transport and Road Research Laboratory (DoE)	Library ordering, catalogue laon	o	12,000	10Mb	Prime 400 (512kb)
	Integration with Int. database	d	60,000	150Mb	
	Ongoing research database	o	10,000	20Mb	
	Computer programs database	o	200		
UKAEA Culham Laboratory	Database of results of Fusion R&D	p		10Mb	2 × ICL2976 (8Mb)
	Library database on plasma physics	p		50Mb	
UKAEA Harwell Laboratory	Library Loan Control System	o	3,000	1.5Mb	IBM 3033 (8Mb)
	Customer Information System	o	30,000	10Mb	

*Status: o = operational; d = active development; p = planned database.

APPENDIX II

COMPARISON OF INPUT FORMATS

Note, that these examples are intended only to give a flavour of various input formats and are not complete and correct in all details.

STATUS input
    ££T
    ££N TITLE
    Guidelines for the use of hearing tests in the Medical Research Council
    ££N AUTHOR
    John Ian Beveridge
    ££T
    ££N PUBLISHER
    Allen and Unwin, London <
    #DATE 1978
    ££N CLASS
    561.72
    ££N COLLATION
    429 p.   22 cms.
    ££A

MARC input

	Tag	*Field*
(Class)	0.82	561.72
(Author)	100.10	Beveridge $h John $f Ian #
(Title)	245.10	Guidelines for the use of hearing tests in the Medical Research Council #
(Imprint)	260	London $b Allen and Unwin $c 1978 #
(Collation)	300	429 p. #c 22 cms. #

APPENDIX III

COMPARISON OF SAMPLE SESSION

Note, that these examples are intended only to give a flavour of various types of search system and are not complete and correct in all details.

UCI (MENU) SYSTEM
Each block represents a full screen menu, the user choices are shown in bold type.

```
                    Available Functions
        A  —  Author Search
        B  —  Subject Search
        C  —  Title Search
        H  —  Help
        E  —  Exit

        Enter option b
```

```
                 Subject Search Mode
                        Subject

            ┌─────────────────────────────┐
            │         hearing             │
            └─────────────────────────────┘

        Press ENTER KEY after entering all field.
```

```
                    Subject Posting
            Ref #      Entries        Subject
            R101         356      Health Surveys
            R102         159      Hearing
            R103          59      Hearing Aids
            R104         288      Hearing Disorders
            R105          72      Hearing Tests
            R106         257      Heart
        Enter Ref # or E to exit r105
```

> 561.72
>
> Beveridge, John Ian
>
> **Guidelines for the application of hearing tests in the Medical Research Council**
>
> Allen and Unwin, London
> 429 p.   22 cms.

STATUS (command) system

All user commands are entered in response to the system prompt >

> > **Q Hearing tests @ title ?**
> > Question is satisfied by 72 articles
>
> > **D**
> > TITLE
> > Guidelines for the application of hearing tests in the Medical Research Council
> > AUTHOR
> > John Ian Beveridge
> > PUBLISHER
> > Allen and Unwin, London
> > # DATE 1978
> > CLASS
> > 561.72
> > COLLATION
> > 429 p.   22 cms.

CITE (natural language) system

PLEASE ENTER YOUR SEARCH QUESTION

Use of hearing tests at M.R.C. and other research institutions

5 QUERY TERMS HAVE BEEN PROCESSSED
MAXIMUM DOCUMENT WEIGHT IS: 19

WEIGHT	TERM
1	MRC
2	RESEARCH
4	INSTITUTIONS
5	TESTS
7	HEARING

RECORD NUMBER 1 WEIGHT: 14

TITLE   Guidelines for the application of hearing test in the Medical Research Council

AUTHOR   Beveridge, John Ian

PUBLISHER Allen and Unwin, London 1978

CONTINUE PRINTING (Y/N)? **n**

APPENDIX IV
HIGH FREQUENCY BASIC VOCABULARY

	Word	*Mean Frequency (%)*
1	the	8.4
2	of	6.5
3	to	3.5
4	or	2.7
5	in	2.6
6	and	2.3
7	be	1.6
8	any	1.6
9	by	1.5
10	a	1.5
11	shall	1.5
12	for	1.2
13	as	1.1
14	this	1.1
15	such	0.89
16	that	0.78
17	under	0.67
18	which	0.66
19	is	0.65
20	many	0.65
21	on	0.61
22	with	0.54
23	not	0.50
24	an	0.43
25	if	0.40
26	other	0.40
27	it	0.34
28	have	0.31
29	from	0.29
30	made	0.28
31	been	0.27
32	at	0.26
33	where	0.25
34	so	0.25
35	has	0.23
36	are	0.21
37	his	0.19
38	all	0.18
	TOTAL	47.3%

Index